Beginner's Guide to
Knitting

To my three boys: Simon,
Tom and Sam.

Beginner's Guide to
Knitting

Alison Dupernex

SEARCH PRESS

UNICORN
BOOKS AND CRAFTS, INC.

First published in Great Britain 2004

Search Press Limited
Wellwood, North Farm Road,
Tunbridge Wells, Kent TN2 3DR

and in the United States of America in association with

Unicorn Books & Crafts Inc
1338 Ross Street
Petaluma
CA 94954-6502

ISBN 1 903975 83 2

Suppliers
If you have difficulty in obtaining any of the materials and
equipment mentioned in this book, then please write to the
Publishers, at the address above, for a current list of stockists,
including firms who operate a mail-order service.

Publisher's note
All the step-by-step photographs in this book
feature the author, Alison Dupernex, demonstrating
knitting. No models have been used.

Colour separation by Classicscan Pte Ltd, Singapore
Printed in Malaysia by Times Offset (M) Sdn Bhd

*My thanks to Ann Hinchliffe from Rowan who kept
up with my demand for yarn; Anita Charman, Anne
Budworth and Diane Davis for helping out with the
knitting, and Pauline Horton for typing. Thanks also
to the team at Search Press: my editor Ally, to Juan
for the design, to Rachel for producing the charts and
to Val for even more typing. Last but not least,
thanks to Roddy for the photographs.*

Page 1

Simple Stripes
*The basic sweater (see page 42) worked in stripes, and
the square hat (see page 78) make a winning
combination.*

Page 3

Comfy Cushions
*The basic cushion (see page 30) and a variation in
different shades of the same yarn.*

Contents

Introduction

Over the years, the popularity of hand knitting has waxed and waned. Until recently it was definitely on the wane; there were few new knitters and the skills traditionally passed from mother to daughter were being lost. But now it is undergoing a dramatic revival, shaking off its 'homespun' reputation, and a new generation is discovering its delights. It is always a staple in the collections of top designers, and its growing popularity is underscored by celebrity knitters like Julia Roberts.

Learning to knit gives you freedom of choice. Instead of buying one of many identical items, you can choose the shade, design and style, adjust measurements or sleeve length, and make something that is completely individual. The choice of yarns and patterns is inspiring, and in a busy world knitting is also great therapy. It can be done almost anywhere: members of *Cast Off,* a group of 'guerilla knitters', take their work on the London Underground and encourage passengers to join in!

Today, knitting is regarded as a leisure activity, but this was not always the case. It was developed in Arab countries, and spread through trade with other nations. In medieval times, religious orders established knitting as a vital skill, and by the 16th century a profitable living could be made from knitting. The first knitting frame was established in the 1580s by clergyman William Lee, and a huge hosiery industry was established. Hand knitting became a cottage industry, and whole families joined in with the carding and spinning. This was knitting's most creative period, during which wonderful, rich patterns were devised. Families designed their own patterns which became so recognisable that a fisherman could be identified by his sweater.

During the last century, knitting became an enjoyable hobby as well as a way of clothing the family, until the pace of leisure life accelerated and it began to be seen as old-fashioned and fuddy-duddy. Not any more! Now, the joys of knitting can be experienced by all. The instructions in this book are designed with the beginner in mind. The styles are easy-to-wear, simple shapes in yarns that will inspire you. Some projects can be completed in a weekend, while others are ideal for winter evenings by the fire. Start with a scarf, work through the projects you like and by the end of the book you will be a competent knitter. Above all, enjoy your knitting as much as I do.

Alison

Knitting bag
A wonderful variety of scarves, hats and sweaters for people of all ages.

Materials

No expensive equipment is needed for knitting. Take two needles and some yarn, cast on a few stitches and you are off. You will probably have basic sewing equipment around the house, and you can collect a few little extras to help to make your life easier as you gain more experience. It is best to buy new needles when you start to knit. Old needles may be chipped or bent out of shape and could snag on your yarn or make the rows uneven.

Buttons
Always choose your buttons with your yarn so you know what size buttonholes to make. With natural yarns like wool or silk, I like to use buttons made of natural materials like wood, shell or leather.

Drawing materials
You will need these if you want to design motifs to add to your knitting. I use squared or graph paper to plan out simple designs, letting one square represent one stitch. I sketch out the design in pencil, and when I am happy with it I add the colour using felt-tipped pens. I then follow my chart to add the motifs using the Swiss Darning technique. See page 58 for more information.

Double-ended cable needle This is used to move a few stitches to the front or back of the work, changing the sequence of the stitches so cable patterns can be produced.

Stitch holder Use this to hold stitches out of the way so that another section of the garment, such as a neckband, can be worked.

Needle gauge This measures the size of the needle and shows equivalent metric, US and imperial sizes.

Circular needle These are made from lengths of plastic wire ending in short needles. They are particularly useful when you are working lots of stitches, or working in the round without a seam.

Crochet hooks Keep a few of these in different sizes to pick up dropped stitches. They are also useful to produce a quick edging.

Knitting needles I prefer metal needles as they are smooth, strong and light. Plastic and bamboo are becoming fashionable, but they bend and are not so easy to use. To avoid splitting the yarn, choose needles with blunt ends.

Row counter Slip this on the end of the needle when working cables and stitch patterns, and alter the count every time a row is worked.

Sewing needles You will need blunt-ended or tapestry needles in a variety of sizes for different yarn thicknesses.

Tape measure To compare measurements on tension (gauge) squares, it is best if this is marked in both centimetres and inches.

Scissors Keep these just for knitting and sewing as cutting paper will blunt them.

Pins Glass-headed pins are ideal as the heat of an iron will not melt them if they are used for blocking. The brightly coloured heads help to ensure that they are not left in the work after sewing up.

Yarns

A huge selection of yarn is available in an amazing range of colours, textures and thicknesses. Yarn for knitting can be bought in balls, on cones or in hanks. If you buy yarn in hanks you should wind it into balls before you start to knit.

Smooth yarn will show up a stitch pattern better. There are also novelty, fun yarns which may be multicoloured, random dyed, or change from thick to thin. Some look like spaghetti and some even look like fake fur! These yarns are better when they are used for a design without a stitch pattern as the interest is in the yarn itself.

When you start to knit, choose a yarn that you are enthusiastic about and that you will enjoy working with. Never begin with an old ball of yarn that someone has given you, or something that you have picked up cheaply: buy the best you can afford. If you cannot find a yarn that is featured in this book, do not panic – you can substitute another as long as you check the tension (gauge) given carefully and make sure you achieve the same measurements with the substitute yarn.

Coned yarn is often used by machine knitters, but it is also suitable for hand knitting and is an inexpensive way to buy yarn.

Yarn weights		Needle sizes		
UK	US	Universal	US	UK*
4 ply	Sport	3mm	2–3	11
Double Knitting	Light Worsted	4mm	6	8
Aran	Fisherman	5mm	8	6
Chunky	Bulky	6mm	10	4
Super Chunky	Extra Bulky	9mm	13	00

* Old UK sizes for needles are included for guidance, but these are no longer manufactured

Large needles look fun but can be cumbersome to use. The work will grow quickly, but it is difficult to hold the needles and yarn in your hands at the same time. I suggest that you start off with a double knitting (light worsted) yarn and 4mm (US 6) needles.

Essentials

If you've never knitted anything before, these pages may look daunting – but do not worry. All the information you will need to develop your knitting skills is here, and everything will become clear very soon. The techniques are clearly explained in the order that you will need to know them, and for clarity all techniques pages are pale blue.

The list opposite contains the abbreviations you will find in this book, plus the most common ones used in knitting instructions. You will find it useful to refer to as you work through the book, but you will not need it for the first project, a simple but effective scarf in easy garter stitch.

Start by buying a pair of nice new needles and a yarn you really like: you will only need six balls, so treat yourself. Do not be tempted to use old needles you have lying around: they may be scratched or bent, which could affect the quality of your knitting. The needles and yarn used in the first project are those I always recommend to beginners: 4mm (US 6) and double knitting (light worsted) weight. The needle chart opposite gives approximate equivalents in metric, US and old UK sizes, but you will not need it until you have learned the basics. For most knitting you will not need anything smaller than 3mm (US 2 or 3) or bigger than 9mm (US 13), though the Razzle-Dazzle scarf on page 28 is made on huge needles. Note that some knitting terms are not universal: these are also explained in the chart opposite.

Make sure you are in a warm room, as you will find your fingers do not work as well when they are cold. Sit in a good light or, better still, in natural daylight. That's it, really – so what are you waiting for? Make a start!

Ball band

This is important, so do not throw it away until you have completed the garment. A ball band provides you with a great deal of information about the yarn it contains, including details of the manufacturer, the weight of the yarn and what it is made from, (for example 100% merino wool), the shade name and/or number, the dye batch number, the size of needles the manufacturer recommends, and the tension or gauge you should achieve. It will also include washing instructions in an international code.

You will find these instructions on your ball band

5/40°	Machine/hand wash warm (40C) Medium machine wash, normal rinse and spin Do not rub or wring Dry flat
6/40°	Machine/hand wash warm (40C) Minimum machine wash, cold rinse, short spin. Do not wring
7/40°	Machine/hand wash warm (40C) Minimum machine wash, spin. Do not rub or wring Dry flat
(hand symbol)	Hand wash only warm (40C) Do not rub or wring. Dry flat
(crossed triangle)	Do not bleach

(iron, one dot)	Cool iron
(iron, two dots)	Warm iron
(iron, three dots)	Hot iron
(crossed iron)	Do not iron
(crossed circle-in-square)	Dry-clean only
(A)	Dry-cleanable in all solvents
(P)	Dry-cleanable in certain solvents; consult cleaner
(crossed circle)	Do not dry-clean

Abbreviations

These are common terms that are used in this book and in knitting instructions generally

alt alternate
approx approximately
beg beginning
CF cable forward
CB cable back
cm centimetres
cont continue
DK Double Knitting (US Light Worsted)
dec decrease by working two stitches together
dpn double pointed needle
foll following
g gramme(s)
inc increase (the most usual way to do this is to work into the front and the back of the stitch)
in inches
K/k knit
knitwise by knitting the stitch
K2tog knit the next two stitches together
LH/lh left hand
M1/m1 make one stitch by picking up the loop between two stitches and working into the back of it
no number
P/p purl
PSSO/psso pass slipped stitch over
purlwise by purling the stitch
P2tog purl two stitches together
rem remain/remaining
rep repeat
RH right hand
RS/rs right side
SS/ss stocking or stockinette stitch
sl slip a stitch
st(s) stitch(es)
tbl through the back of the loop
tog together
WS/ws wrong side
YO/yo yarn over needle to make a stitch
YRN/yrn yarn round needle
* used to mark the beginning of pattern repeats
( ) used to enclose larger sizes / certain instructions

Needle sizes

US	Universal (mm)	UK*
0	2	14
1	2.25	13
2	2.75	12
–	3	11
3	3.25	10
4	3.5	–
5	3.75	9
6	4	8
7	4.5	7
8	5	6
9	5.5	5
10	6	4
–	6.5	3
–	7	2
–	7.5	1
11	8	0
13	9	00
15	10	000
17	12.5	n/a
19	15	n/a
35	19	n/a
36	20	n/a

Note: equivalents should not be regarded as exact. Where they fall between sizes, dashes have been used. Check your tension or gauge before you start.

* Old UK sizes for needles are included for guidance, but these are no longer manufactured.

Variations in terms

UK	US
cast off	bind off
stocking stitch	stockinette stitch
tension	gauge

CHOOSING THE RIGHT NEEDLES

Every knitting pattern includes advice on how to check whether the stitches you produce are the correct tension or gauge. New knitters may think this is boring and unnecessary, but it is one of the most important things you can do if you want to achieve good results. Just a tiny variation from the stitch tension or gauge stated can make a huge difference to the size of your finished garment.

To check your tension or gauge, count the stitches across and down your work carefully, using pins to mark out the area you want to measure.

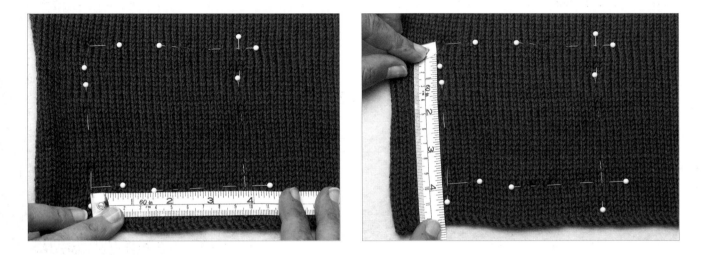

WORKING A SAMPLE SWATCH

Check your tension or gauge carefully by working a sample swatch before you begin, then you can change your needle size if necessary. Your pattern will often tell you to work the sample in stockinette stitch as this is far easier to measure. The samples below were made in double knitting weight yarn using needles in sizes 3, 4 and 5mm (US 3, 6 and 8).

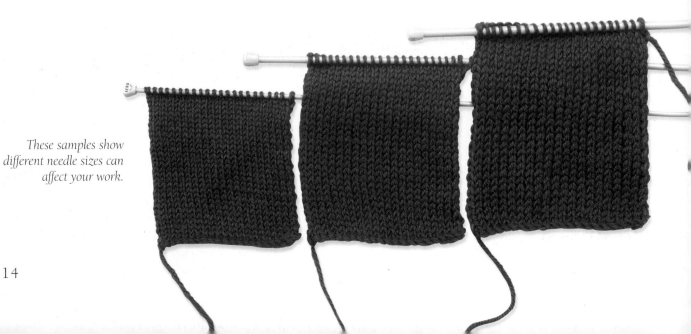

These samples show different needle sizes can affect your work.

BLOCKING AND PRESSING

Before you sew the pieces together you should block and press them. This will reshape the item if it has lost its shape, smooth out the stitches and help to prevent the edges from rolling, which will make it easier to sew up. Some knitted fabrics, such as garter stitch, only need blocking and not pressing.

BLOCKING

You can use a blanket or towel, but the best thing to use is the wrong side of heat-resistant fabric that is made to protect tables. Cover this with cotton fabric. Lay each piece of work on the fabric and check the measurements with a tape measure, easing it a little if necessary. Place pins at intervals of 1–1½in (2–3cm), making sure that the side edges are the same length and that both sleeves match. Ribbing should not be pinned as it needs to remain springy. Make sure all the rows of knitting run parallel. Fill a spray bottle with water and spray the knitted pieces lightly. Allow them to dry thoroughly. Be patient, as this may take a whole day.

Place pins at intervals of 1–1½in (2–3cm)

PRESSING

Check the ball band to see if the manufacturers advise pressing. As a guide, man-made yarns such as nylon or acrylic should not be pressed as they go limp and lose their shape. Wool, cotton, silk or mixtures of these can be pressed lightly.

Lay out the pieces as for blocking and heat your iron to the required temperature. There are two ways to press your work. One is to cover it with a damp cloth and use an iron on a normal setting, working it very gently over the pieces with a waving movement. The other is to use a dry cloth and an iron set to steam, allowing the steam to pass through the cloth on to the work. Leave the pieces to dry thoroughly before you remove them.

Note
Use striped or checked material under your work. It will help you to keep a straight line, and ensure that you do not distort the work while pressing.

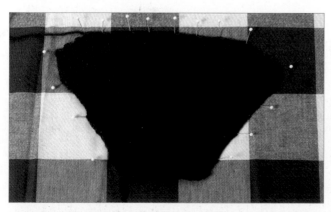

Pin your work out as for blocking

Never slide the iron across the surface of the pressing cloth

Making a start

These pages will help you through the basics of knitting. Once you know them, you will be building on a firm foundation: most of the infinite variety of stitches start with these basics. At first the needles will feel strange in your hands and the yarn will never be where you need it, but keep calm and don't panic. If you find you are becoming frustrated, leave your work for a few minutes and go and do something else. When you come back, suddenly everything will make sense. In time, the needles and yarn will become an extension of your hands.

Note
Before you begin to knit, try to relax. If you are stressed or tense, your knitting will be too tight.

CASTING ON

Casting on – putting stitches on to your needle – is the basis of your knitting. There are several different methods, and I have shown the two most popular. The two-needle method shown opposite gives a firm, neat edge.

SLIP KNOT

A slip knot is very useful and you should learn to make one before you begin. It is very easy to tighten, and if it goes wrong you simply slip it off the needle and pull both ends. It will come undone without leaving a knot in the yarn.

1 Wind the yarn into a loop …

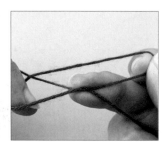
2 …and bring the short end underneath.

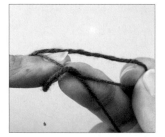
3 Pull the strand up…

4 …and through the loop.

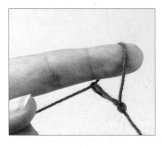
5 Gently tighten the loop at the base…

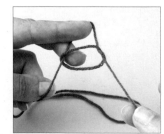
6 …so the knot is ready to insert the needle.

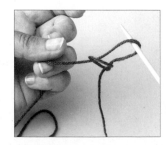
7 Insert the needle and pull gently on one end so the knot closes.

8 The first stitch is on the needle.

TWO-NEEDLE CAST-ON

1 Insert the right needle in the loop on the left needle.

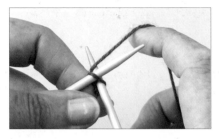

2 Wrap the yarn round the right needle.

3 Pick up the loop of yarn...

4 ...and pull it through.

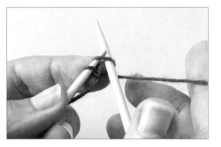

5 Place the stitch on the left needle and pull the yarn gently to close the loop. Do not pull it too tight.

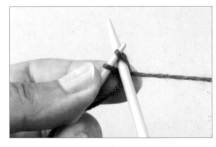

6 Insert the right needle between the two cast-on stitches.

7 Take the yarn over the needle as before...

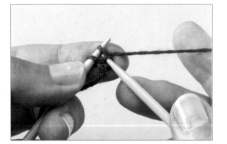

8 ...and pull the loop through...

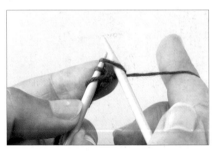

9 ...then place it on the left needle.

THUMB METHOD

This method of casting on uses only one needle. It is not quite as neat as the basic cast-on, but it gives an elastic edge that is particularly useful for hats.

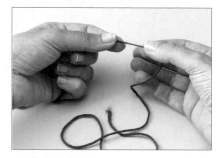

1 From your ball of yarn, measure off about ¾in (2cm) for each stitch that you want to cast on.

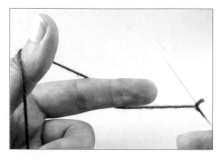

2 Make a slip knot a little further on and place the loop on the needle. Hold the needle and yarn from the ball in your right hand.

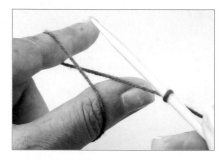

3 Wind the free end of the yarn round the thumb and forefinger of your left hand and hold it in place with your remaining fingers.

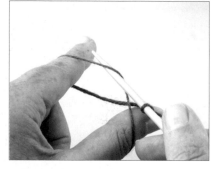

4 Insert the needle into the loop on your forefinger...

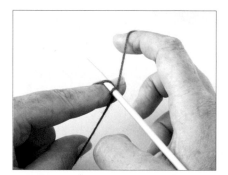

5 ...and pull the end of the yarn to close the loop. Take the yarn from the ball over your right forefinger...

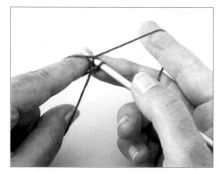

6 ...and anti-clockwise round the point of the needle.

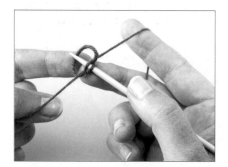

7 Ease the loop on your left forefinger over the point of the needle, slipping your finger out at the same time...

8 ...and tighten the yarn gently.

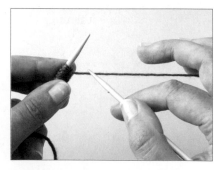

9. Repeat steps 3–8 to cast on the next stitch.

GARTER STITCH

Garter stitch is the easiest to begin with as you simply knit every stitch in every row. It is a versatile stitch which is suitable for any yarn and is the same on both the front and back. The texture has ridges and is elastic. You will soon get into the rhythm you need to produce even garter stitch. It is also called knit stitch, which is abbreviated to K.

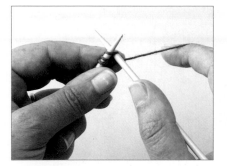

1 Insert the point of the right needle in the front of the first stitch.

2 Hold the yarn in the right hand as shown below. Take it over the right needle with your forefinger...

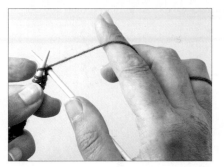

3 ...and between the needles...

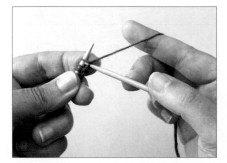

4 ...then use the point of the right needle to pick up the yarn between the needles and pull it through...

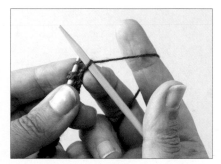

5 ...making a loop on the right needle. At the same time, lift the stitch over the left needle...

6 ...and drop it. You have now worked one stitch and are ready to work the next in the same way.

HOLDING THE YARN

There are many ways to hold the yarn and this is mine, but in time you may devise your own. The yarn is threaded over the third finger of the right hand to tighten it as it is being worked. This helps to ensure that you work to the correct tension or gauge.

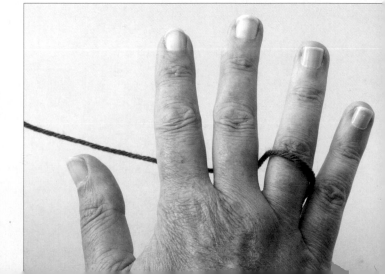

STOCKINETTE STITCH

Garter stitch has ridges, but stockinette stitch is smooth on one side and ridged on the other. To make a stockinette fabric, knit one row and purl back again, then repeat the process. It will not take long to get into the rhythm and it will become clear whether you are on a knit or a purl row.

THE PURL STITCH

1 Insert the right needle in the first stitch on the left needle, with the point in front of your work.

2 Take the yarn over...

3 ...and loop it around the right needle.

4 Draw the loop through the stitch on the left needle...

5 ...so that the yarn is at the front of the work.

6 ...and complete by slipping the stitch off the left needle...

7 ...on to the right needle.

8 Repeat steps 1–7 to the end of the row.

9 Turn your work over and knit the next row as for garter stitch (see page 19). Repeat the last two rows as many times as you need.

FASTENING OFF YOUR WORK

When you have completed your piece of work, it must be finished off to prevent it unravelling. This is called casting off or binding off. The stitches are linked together along the edge of the work. The method used here resembles a chain. If you need a loosely cast off edge, round a neck for example, use a larger size needle. You can also cast off in rib by working *K1, P1, pass the knit stitch over the purl stitch. Repeat from * to the end of the row.

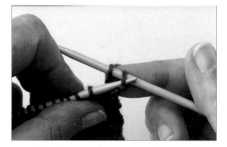

1 Knit two stitches. Insert the point of the left needle, left to right, into the first stitch...

2 ...lift it up...

3 ...and drop it over the first stitch.

4 Repeat the process all the way along the row.

5 Leave the last loop on the needle and cut the yarn, leaving a long end.

6 Thread the long end of yarn through the loop...

7 ...and pull the end gently through the loop to fasten off.

Note
When you are counting garter stitch, each ridge counts as two rows. Alternate ridges are on the other side of the work and cannot be seen.

PICKING UP A DROPPED STITCH

Garter stitch produces a firm fabric and dropped stitches may not run down very far. If you drop a stitch when you are working in garter stitch and notice before it runs down your work, you can pick it up with one of your knitting needles. You can also pick up dropped stitches with a crochet hook – see the method opposite.

1 Identify the dropped stitch, which should look like a loop over the top of the stitch below.

2 Ease out the loop of the dropped stitch so it is big enough to insert your needle.

3 Pick it up with the left needle. Use the right needle to pick up the stitch below, *behind* the dropped stitch.

4 Place it on the left needle, then use the point of the needle to...

5 ...pick up the unravelled stitch and work it through...

6 ...and on to the right needle.

7 Transfer the stitch back to the left needle and work it. Make sure your work looks neat and continue with the row.

Note

If a stitch runs down several rows, use a crochet hook to pick it up – see opposite. This is slightly more difficult with garter stitch as you will have to change the direction of the hook on each row.

DROPPED STITCH IN STOCKINETTE FABRIC

If you drop a stitch when you are working in stockinette stitch and do not notice for some time, it can run down and cause a ladder in your work. If this happens, you will find it easier to pick up the dropped stitches with a crochet hook. Pick up the stitch with the right side of your work facing.

1 Hold your work firmly beneath the dropped stitch so it does not run down any more.

2 Insert a crochet hook into the loop of the dropped stitch.

3 Slide the hook through the loop and hook it under the strand of yarn above the stitch.

4 Catch the strand with the hook and pull it through the loop.

5 Repeat the procedure with the next strand of yarn...

6 ...and continue until you have picked up all the dropped stitches.

7 Place the stitch back on the left needle.

Super Scarves

The easiest project to start with is a garter stitch scarf. All you need to do is cast on, work rows until the scarf is long enough, then cast off. Count your stitches often to make sure you have not lost or gained any! Instructions for finishing the scarf are on pages 26–27.

Simply Snuggly

This simple method is the basis for lots of variations: you can have endless fun embellishing your finished scarf with fringes or even pompoms (see page 82). For even more fun, make a stripy scarf. When you have completed these first projects, move on to the scarves later in the section.

Plain scarf

Using 4mm (US 6) needles and the two needle method (see page 17) cast on 60 sts and work in garter stitch (every row knit) until the scarf measures 68in (170cm). Cast off loosely.

Stripy scarf

Using 4mm (US 6) needles, A and the two needle method, cast on 60 sts and work 30 rows of garter st.
Second stripe: change to B and work 30 rows.
Third stripe: change to C and work 30 rows.
Fourth stripe: change to D and work 30 rows.
Fifth stripe: change to E and work 30 rows.
Repeat stripes in colour sequence until the scarf measures 68in (170cm) and you are at the end of a 30-row section. Cast off loosely.

You will need

Single-colour scarf

Jaeger Matchmaker Merino DK (50g balls): 6 balls of Flax (893)

Stripy scarf

Jaeger Matchmaker Merino DK (50g balls), 2 balls of:
A Flax (893)
and 1 ball each of:
B Putty (892)
C Azalea (897)
D Pearl (891)
E Geranium (894)

For both scarves

4mm (US 6) needles

Tapestry needle for sewing in the yarn ends

Cardboard template 4in (12.5cm) square for tassels

Crochet hook for tassels

Tape measure

Tension (gauge): 22 sts and 44 rows to 4in (10cm)

Measurements: width 11½in (29cm); length 68in (170cm)

Work in progress
Garter stitch can look very attractive once you find a rhythm and begin to produce even rows.

Opposite

The finished scarves
Tassels have been added to both ends, spaced about ¾in (2cm) apart

ADDING DIFFERENT COLOURS

Striped scarves may look complicated, but are actually very easy. Simply break off one yarn at the end of a row and start working with another. The ends are sewn in when you have finished the scarf.

Break the yarn at the end of a row and work with another colour.

The right side of the work

The wrong side of the work

SEWING IN THE ENDS

Take a little time to do this as finishing is important for a neat project. Thread the ends of the yarn on to a tapestry needle with a large eye and a blunt tip. Take them down the edge of the scarf (see below), never into the work as this will look untidy. Trim the ends after sewing them in.

Working the threaded needle in and out of the scarf edge.

Trimming the ends after sewing in

Note
Never join yarn in the middle of a row, even if it is the same shade. It will not look neat and will always leave a bulge.

Striped scarf
When finishing the striped scarf make sure you sew all the ends in down the side of the corresponding colour.

MAKING A FRINGE

A fringe finishes off the scarf and adds another texture to the project. You can make a long or short fringe, depending on the size of the card template, but keep it in proportion: a small scarf needs a short fringe. I used a 5in (12.5cm) template.

1 Wrap the yarn closely round the card template.

2 Cut through the yarn on one side only.

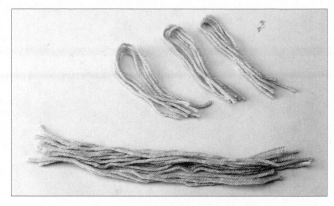

3 Divide the cut yarn into bunches of eight strands and fold each in half to make one section of fringe.

4 With a crochet hook, draw a section of fringe through the scarf edge...

5...to make a loop. Bring the cut strands of yarn over the hook...

6 ...and pull them through the loop.

7 Pull the cut ends of the yarn gently to secure.

8 Repeat along the scarf edge, making sure each piece of fringe is attached in the same way.

The fringe on the striped scarf is added in the same way but using colours in the same sequence as the stripes.

27

USING NOVELTY YARN

There are so many novelty yarns on the market. The two I have used here are both fashionable and easy to work with. Rowan Denim shrinks in length when it is washed and fades slightly, which emphasises the texture of the garter stitch. The tassel fringing frays, which immediately makes the scarf feel like an old friend. Rowan Biggy Print is a heavily-textured yarn in a range of bright colours for a real razzle-dazzle look.

Blue Jeans

Using the thumb method and 4mm (US 6) needles, cast on 60 sts and work in garter st until work measures 59in (150cm). Cast off loosely. Cut 7in (15cm) lengths of yarn and make enough six-strand tassels to place one every 10 rows up the sides and every 10 sts across the lower edge.

Razzle-Dazzle

Using 20mm (US 36) needles and the thumb method, cast on 18 sts. Knit until work measures 62in (170cm) without pulling or stretching. Cast off loosely. Gather in the lower edge by threading a needle with the yarn and weaving it in and out. Draw together and fasten off. Cut eight 9½in (24cm) lengths of yarn, fold in half, tie with spare yarn and sew to the end of the scarf. Repeat with the other end of the scarf.

You will need

Blue Jeans scarf

Rowan Denim (50g balls): 6 balls of Tennessee (231)

4mm (US 6) needles

Crochet hook for tassels

Tension (gauge): 20 sts and 28 rows to 4in (10cm) before washing

Measurements: 12 x 59in (30 x 150cm) excluding fringe

Razzle-Dazzle scarf

Rowan Biggy Print (100g balls): 6 balls of Fiesta (251)

20mm (US 36) needles

Tension (gauge): 5½ sts and 7 rows to 4in (10cm)

Measurements: 12 x 62in (30 x 158cm) excluding tassel

For both scarves:

Tapestry needle to sew in the yarn ends

Tape measure

Detail of the tassels on the Denim scarf, after washing.

Detail of the gathered end and tassel on the Biggy Print scarf.

Opposite

The finished scarves

28

Pretty 'Patchwork'

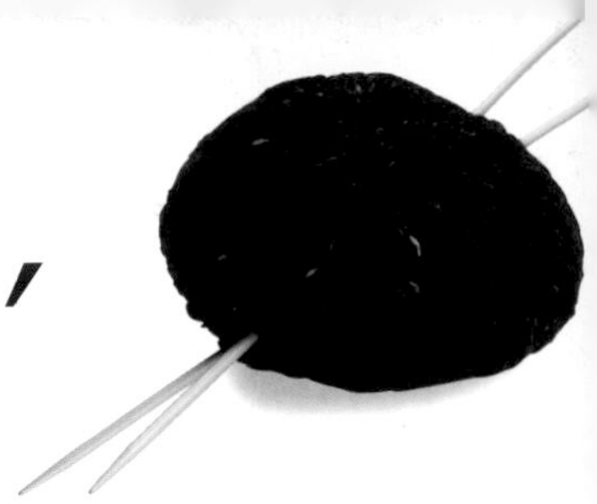

These knitted 'patchwork' projects may look complicated, but they are so easy. They are worked in strips of stockinette stitch with different colours joined in at intervals along the length. When the strips are sewn together the sequence of the sections of knitting produces an extremely convincing patchwork effect.

Comfy Cushion

The instructions for this cushion are given in my choice of colours, but you could choose and plan your own. A cushion pad is inserted when you have completed it, and simple tassels added to the corners and back flap to finish it off.

Working the strips

With 4mm (US 6) needles cast on 22 sts and work 30 rows H.
Change to E and work 30 rows.
Follow the colour sequence shown on the chart below until the first strip has been completed. Cast off loosely.
Work strips 2, 3, 4, 5 and 6 in the same way, following the relevant column on the chart.

Strip No.	1	2	3	4	5	6	
	H	C	G	J	B	I	
	E	F	C	B	F	D	
	I	D	G	J	I	E	
	E	F	B	C	F	H	Fold
	L	E	I	H	E	L	
	H	F	B	C	F	E	
	E	D	G	J	D	I	
	A	C	J	G	B	A	Front of cushion
	I	B	G	J	C	H	
	E	F	C	B	F	E	
	L	E	H	I	E	L	Fold
	E	F	C	B	F	E	
	I	B	G	J	C	H	
	A	C	J	G	B	A	
	A	C	J	G	B	A	Overlap
	A	C	J	G	B	A	

Key to order of strips
Follow this chart to produce the cushion shown opposite, or plan your own colours using it as a guide.

You will need

Rowan Felted Tweed (50g balls) 1 ball each of:

A Dragon (147)
B Sigh (148)
C Crush (139)
D Cocoa (143)
E Treacle (145)
F Conker (144)
G Rage (150)
H Bilberry (151)
I Midnight (133)
J Watery (152)
K Phantom (153)
L Whisper (141)

4mm (US 6) needles

Tape measure

Glass-headed pins

Tapestry needle for sewing up

Card template 3in (7.5cm) square for tassels

Cushion pad 20in (50cm)

Iron and padded surface for pressing

Tension (gauge): 22 sts and 30 rows to 4in (10cm)

Measurements: just over 20in (50cm) square

Note
If you want to design your own cushion, each ball of the specified yarn should produce about 12 squares.

The finished cushion
Follow the instructions or substitute your own choice of colours.

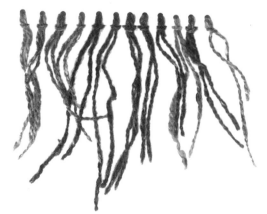

Yarn swatch
When I am using lots of different colours I make a shade card threaded with lengths of the yarn and label them with the letter used to identify them in the key.

FINISHING THE CUSHION

Pressing will make the strips easier to sew together. Before you start to join the strips, press each of them lightly as shown here.

First, lay out a strip flat and cover with a damp cloth. Set the iron to warm and pass it gently over the cloth. Ease the work gently, and take care to press the edges as they are inclined to roll. Remove the damp cloth and allow the work to dry. It can then be handled safely as it will no longer pull out of shape. Press the other strips in the same way.

MAKING UP

Making up is just as important as knitting, so take time to finish off the cushion neatly. Many pieces of knitting are ruined by rushed and careless finishing. There are several ways to join your work, and the method you choose will depend on the finish you want.

To join the strips, I used mattress stitch, which gives a very smooth, almost invisible seam that is also ideal for baby clothes. For the sides, I used back stitch, which is ideal where strength is required. This stitch is also used for shoulder and sleeve seams.

Place the two pieces of work you want to join side by side with the right side of the work uppermost. Thread a needle with a large eye and a blunt tip with the yarn you have used for knitting – a tapestry needle is ideal – and follow the steps below.

> **Note**
> For clarity, a contrast yarn has been used to sew up the knitted strips.

MATTRESS STITCH

1 Secure the yarn to the lower right corner. Take the needle across to the left edge, and under the strand of yarn between the first and second stitches of the first row.

2 Take the needle back to the right edge and insert it one row up, between the first and second stitches of the row.

3 Take the needle back to the left edge and repeat the procedure.

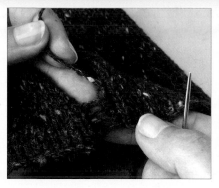

4 When you have completed a few stitches, gently pull up the yarn...

5 ...to close the gap...

6 ...so the seam is neat and almost invisible.

BACK STITCH

Fold the cushion, right sides together, so that it is almost like an envelope. Pin at right angles to the seam so that your stitches can pass over the pins easily.

1 Pin the pieces of work right sides together. Secure the yarn to the beginning of your work, one stitch in from the edge.

2 Take the needle down through both pieces of work and come out two rows to the left.

3 Take the needle to the right and insert it where the previous stitch ended, then take it behind your work to emerge four rows to the left.

4 Pull the yarn gently as you work, but do not pull it too tightly.

5 Close each loop of yarn before beginning the next stitch.

6 Repeat this process all along the seam. To finish, oversew several stitches and cut the thread.

ADDING TASSELS

Tassels are a wonderful embellishment and add a professional touch of luxury to any item. I made tassels from two different shades of Rowan Felted Tweed (Rage and Watery), and attached them to each corner of the cushion and at intervals along the back flap.

1 Cut a 3in (7.5cm) card template and wrap the yarn evenly round it.

2 Loop a double length of the same yarn through to hold it.

3 Turn the template over and snip through the yarn opposite the loop.

4 Ease the yarn off the card and pull up the loop to bind the top.

5 Wrap the tassel about ¾in (2cm) down with a separate piece of yarn.

6 Tie off the ends of the yarn firmly.

7 Thread a needle on to the tied-off ends of yarn and take them down inside the tassel.

8 Trim the tassel so that the ends are even.

9 Thread the needle with the yarn that is still looped through the top of the tassel to attach it to the corner of the cushion as shown.

Note

Sew in the ends down the small seam after the cushion has been sewn together. Turn the completed cushion right side out. Insert a cushion pad snugly in the knitted 'envelope'.

Detail of the tassels used on the back flap of the cushion. They have been attached to the middle of each square and at the end of each square.

Cosy Cover

This useful and attractive cover for a pram or crib is worked in strips of stocking stitch in exactly the same way as for the cushion. Each strip contains seven squares of 22 stitches and 30 rows. When you have completed the strips press them lightly, join them with mattress stitch (see page 32) and sew in the ends.

SWISS DARNING

To embellish the finished cover, I added embroidered hearts using the red shade of Rowan Felted Tweed, Rage (150). Swiss Darning, also known as duplicate stitch, is embroidery that mimics the stitch, but in a contrasting shade – see page 60 for method. The cover was finished with a quick and easy crochet edging in the same red yarn – see the method on page 38. If you prefer not to try crochet, blanket stitch is a simple alternative – see page 39.

Key to placement of strips
Use the chart above for reference when you work the strips and place the Swiss-darned hearts.

You will need

Rowan Felted Tweed (50g balls):
1 ball each of:
A Dragon (147)
B Sigh (148)
C Crush (139)
D Cocoa (143)
E Treacle (145)
F Conker (144)
G Rage (150)
H Bilberry (151)
I Midnight (133)
J Watery (152)
K Corn (136)
L Phantom (153)

4mm (US 6) needles

Crochet hook: 3mm (US D/3)

Tapestry needle for sewing up

Iron and padded surface

Tape measure

Tension (gauge): 23 sts and 32 rows to 4in (10cm)

Measurements: about 28½in (71cm) square including edging

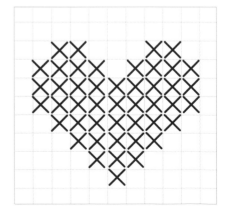

Heart chart
Each cross on the grid represents a stitch. Choose a bold, simple shape for the best effect – the anchor shown on page 61 would look just as good.

The finished cover

This cosy cover would make a practical gift for a new baby. This one was decorated with heart motifs and a matching crochet edging, but you can easily substitute a different motif.

CROCHET EDGING

This is a quick and easy way to give a neat finish to your work (see the pram cover on page 37). Crochet all round the edge of the item in a contrasting yarn, starting with a straight edge. Work three extra stitches at each corner so it lies flat and will not pull.

Detail of crochet edging

1 Insert hook between two stitches, one row in from edge. Yarn over...

2 ...and pull a loop of the yarn through.

3 Insert the crochet hook again, one stitch along...

4 ..and pull the yarn through in a loop again.

5 Pass the yarn over the hook.

6 Gently tighten the yarn in the waist of the hook...

7 ...and pull through the two stitches on the hook...

8 ...to complete a stitch.

9 Insert the hook again two stitches along. Repeat steps 1–8...

10 ...to produce the second stitch.

11 Work in the same way all round the item, inserting three extra stitches on the point of each corner.

BLANKET STITCH

If you do not want to crochet an edging, blanket stitch is an effective substitute and looks good in a contrasting yarn. It can be used for rugs and blankets or even as a decorative touch for the edge of garments. Begin by attaching a contrasting yarn to your work, starting at a corner or edge. So that the finished edge lies flat, take care not to pull the yarn too tight, and work in an extra stitch at each corner.

1 Insert the needle again and wrap the yarn round.

2 Pull the end of the yarn so it loops through.

3 Insert the needle a short distance along and wrap the yarn round the needle as before.

4 Pull the yarn gently to close the stitch.

5 Continue to work the stitch evenly along the edge, spacing the stitches at regular intervals for an even effect.

Tasselled Throw

The strips for this throw are made in exactly the same way as the strips for the cushions. I used Rowan Felted Tweed, but a throw like this is a wonderful way to use up odd scraps of yarn – just make sure they are the same weight and quality.

The strips can be made to a random design, or follow the chart below to make the throw opposite. You may even be feeling confident enough to plan out your own: for guidance, one ball of Felted Tweed should make at least 12 squares.

Complete all the strips, press them, then sew them together with mattress stitch. The finishing touch is added by attaching large tassels, made from equal quantities of Rage (150) and Watery (152), to each corner – see opposite for instructions.

You will need

Rowan Felted Tweed (50g balls)
2 balls each of:

A Dragon (147)
B Sigh (148)
C Crush (139)
D Cocoa (143)
E Treacle (145)
F Conker (144)
G Rage (150)
H Bilberry (151)
I Midnight (133)
J Watery (152)
K Phantom (153)
L Whisper (141)

4mm (US 6) needles

Tapestry needle to sew up the strips

Glass-headed pins

Card for making tassels

Iron and padded surface

Cardboard template 6in (15cm) square

Tape measure

Tension (gauge): 22 sts and 30 rows to 4in (10cm)

Measurements: 60 x 72in (152 x 184cm)

	1	2	3	4	5	6	7	8	9	10	11	12	13	14	15
1	F	D	G	K	I	C	E	C	B	E	I	D	F	G	F
2	J	F	E	H	C	K	D	D	I	K	C	K	J	D	J
3	D	C	K	J	K	D	A	L	A	E	B	C	L	A	D
4	L	I	H	B	D	A	L	H	L	A	E	B	D	K	L
5	C	E	B	D	A	L	H	F	H	L	A	E	I	B	C
6	A	B	D	A	L	H	F	G	F	H	L	A	E	I	A
7	I	H	A	M	H	F	G	J	G	F	H	L	A	E	H
8	L	I	L	H	I	G	J	G	J	G	I	H	L	H	I
9	C	D	H	I	F	I	G	J	G	I	F	I	H	D	E
10	E	B	L	H	I	G	J	G	J	G	I	H	L	I	B
11	B	I	E	L	H	F	G	J	G	F	H	L	A	H	D
12	H	E	B	E	L	H	F	G	F	H	L	A	D	B	E
13	C	A	F	K	E	L	H	F	H	L	A	D	K	I	H
14	D	H	I	C	B	E	L	H	L	A	D	K	I	D	C
15	E	C	J	D	K	H	E	L	A	D	K	B	C	K	E
16	L	B	H	I	E	C	B	E	B	K	C	I	J	A	L
17	I	G	K	B	I	E	C	K	I	L	F	H	G	F	H
18	G	D	F	E	H	K	I	D	B	H	K	C	F	D	G

Key to placement of strips
Use the chart for reference when you are working the strips for the throw.

Note
The edges of this throw have been left plain, but you can finish them off with crochet or blanket stitch if you prefer.

KNOTTING THE CORNER

Make four tassels from a mixture of two shades of yarn. Wind more yarn on the template than for the cushions in the previous project, to keep them in proportion to the throw. Knot the corners as shown before attaching the tassels.

1 Pull the corner firmly...

2 ..and wrap it round your thumb and forefinger.

3 Push the end through.

4 Pull to secure the knot.

Detail of knotted corner

Detail of tassel

Simple Sweater

If you never dreamed you would find yourself tackling a sweater, don't worry – every stage of the process is explained simply on the following pages. While you make the basic sweater, you should learn everything you need to know. Next time you make a sweater, you can make it unique. Swap the ribbing for moss stitch or a rolled edge; add stripes, a motif or a pocket. The choice is yours – you have only to take the plunge.

Perfectly Plain

Note: the first figure given refers to the smallest size. Larger sizes are in brackets, e.g. for size 1 cast on 56 sts; for size 2 cast on 58 sts; for size 3 cast on 64 sts and so on.

Back

Using 3.25mm (US 3) needles cast on 56 (58, 64, 70, 88, 94) sts.
Work 1¼ (1½, 1½, 1½, 2, 2¼)in [3 (4, 4, 4, 5, 6)cm] K1, P1 rib ending with a RS row.
Next row: (inc) P3 (5, 2, 4, 4, 5) M1, P10 (7, 12, 7, 16, 12) to last 3 (4, 2, 3, 4, 5) sts, M1, P3 (4, 2, 3, 4, 5). There should be 62 (66, 70, 80, 94, 102) sts on the needle.
Change to 4mm (US 6) needles and work 40 (50, 50, 66, 72, 80) rows SS, beg with a K row.
Shape armholes: cast off 3 (3, 4, 2, 3, 3) sts at the beg of the next 2 (2, 2, 4, 2, 5) rows. 56 (60, 62, 72, 88, 92) sts rem.**
Work 36 (38, 40, 40, 48, 50) rows SS.
Shape back neck and shoulders:
Sizes 1, 2, 3 and 4
Next row: K13 (15, 16, 17) cast off next 30 (30, 30, 38) sts, K to end.
Next row: P13 (15, 16, 17).
Cast off.
With WS facing, rejoin yarn to rem 13 (15, 16, 17) sts, P to end.
Cast off.
Sizes 5 and 6
Cast off 12 (13) sts, K12 (13) sts, then turn, leaving rem sts on stitch holder.
Next row: P.
Cast off.
With RS facing, rejoin yarn to sts on holder. Cast off centre 40 sts, K to end.
Next row: cast off 12 (13) sts at the beg of the row, P to end.
Cast off.

Instructions continue overleaf

You will need

Jaeger Matchmaker Merino DK (50g balls) in Mariner (629):

Size 1 (6 months) 4 balls
Size 2 (age 1) 4 balls
Size 3 (age 2) 4 balls
Size 4 (age 4) 6 balls
Size 5 (age 6) 7 balls
Size 6 (age 8) 7 balls

4mm (US 6) and 3.25mm (US 3) needles

Stitch holder

Tapestry needle for sewing up

Glass-headed pins

Iron and padded surface

Tape measure

Size 1 only: 2 small buttons and thread to match yarn

Tension (gauge): 22 sts and 30 rows to 4in (10cm) measured over SS on 4mm (US 6) needles.

Note

Ages given are for guidance, so check the chest measurement of the child. All round under the arms, size 1 measures about 22in (56cm), size 2 about 24in (61cm), size 3 about 26in (66cm), size 4 about 2in (71cm), size 5 about 30in (76cm) and size 6 about 32in (81cm). Lengthen or shorten sleeves or side seams by working more or fewer rows straight after making any increases.

The finished sweater
Every child needs one of these simple sweaters in his or her wardrobe – why not make one for your favourite youngster? The first size would make a perfect gift for a special new baby.

Note
It is a good idea to highlight the set of instructions you want to use. If you want to make a different size later, you can do the same with a different shade of highlighter. Photocopy the instructions if you do not want to mark your book.

Front

Work as for Back to **.
Work a further 26 (26, 26, 24, 32, 34) rows SS.
Left neck shaping: K20 (23, 24, 28, 36, 38) sts and turn, leaving rem sts on a stitch holder.

Sizes 1, 2, 3 and 4:
Next and foll alt rows: at neck edge, cast off 3 sts 1 (2, 2, 3) times, 2 sts 1 (0, 0, 1) time and 1 st 2 (2, 2, 0) times so there are 13 (15, 16, 17) sts on your needle. Work 4 (8, 8, 10) rows straight. Cast off.
Right neck shaping: with RS facing, return to sts on holder. Leave centre 16 (14, 14, 16) sts on holder, rejoin yarn to rem sts and work to end. Complete to match left neck, reversing all shapings.

Sizes 5 and 6:
Next and foll 3 alt rows: cast off 3 sts at neck edge, work to end.
Next row: cast off 2 sts at neck edge, work to end.
Next row: cast off 1 st at neck edge, work to end. There should be 24 (26) on your needle.
Work 6 rows without shaping, ending with WS row.
Next row: cast off 12 (13) sts, work to end.
Next row: work to end. Cast off rem 12 (13) sts.
Right neck shaping: with RS facing, return to sts on holder. Leave centre 16 sts on holder, rejoin yarn to rem sts, K to end. Complete to match left neck, reversing all shapings.

Sleeves (both alike)

Using 3.25mm (US 3) needles, cast on 26 (26, 36, 36, 38, 42) sts. Work 1¼ (1½, 1½, 1½, 2¼)in [3 (4, 4, 4, 5, 6) cm] K1, P1 rib.
Next row: inc 4 (4, 0, 0, 2, 2) sts evenly across row. There should be 30 (30, 36, 36, 40, 44) sts on needle. Change to No. 4mm (US 6) needles and work 34 (36, 54, 62, 70, 78) rows SS. *At the same time* shape sleeves by inc 1 st each end of the 3rd (3rd, 4th, 4th, 4th, 4th) row and every foll 2nd (2nd, 3rd, 3rd, 3rd, 3rd) row until there are 56 (64, 56, 56, 60, 64) sts on the needle.
Sizes 3, 4, 5 and 6 only: inc 1 st each end of every 4th row. There should be 64 (64, 72, 78) sts on the needle.
Shape top of sleeve:
Size 1: cast off 3 sts at the beg of the next 6 rows. Cast off rem 38 sts.
Size 2: over the next 10 rows, at the beg of the row cast off 7 sts (twice), 3 sts (twice), 2 sts (4 times) and 5 sts (twice). Cast off rem 26 sts.
Sizes 3 and 4: over the next 10 rows, at the beg of the row, cast off 4 sts (twice), 3 sts (4 times), and 4 sts (4 times). Cast off rem 28 sts.

Sizes 5 and 6: over the next 12 rows, at the beg of the row, cast off 5 sts (twice), 3 sts (8 times) and 5 sts (twice). Cast off rem 28 (34) sts.

Blocking and pressing

Block and press all the pieces. Do not press the ribbing or it will lose its elasticity.

Neckband

Join the right shoulder seam using back stitch. Using pins inserted at right angles, divide the neck edge into equal sections. This will help you to pick up and make stitches evenly around the neck edge.
With RS facing and 3.25mm (US 3) needles pick up 14 (19, 19, 18, 19, 19) sts down left side of front neck, then pick up centre 16 (14, 14, 16, 16, 16) sts from the holder and 14 (19, 19, 18, 19, 19) sts up the right side of the front neck, including 1st from shoulder seam and 29 (29, 29, 37, 39, 39) sts from the back neck. There should be 74 (82, 82, 90, 94, 94) sts on the needle.
Work 1¼in (3cm) K1, P1 rib.
Cast off in rib (see page 50).

Note: if you use a needle one size larger to cast off, the neckband will be easier to pull over the head.

Shoulder opening

As babies' heads are large in proportion to their bodies, you might like to add a shoulder opening for ease of dressing. To do this, first join the left shoulder for 2cm (¾in) at the armhole edge. With RS facing and 3.25mm (US 3) needles, pick up 16 sts across neckband and left back shoulder, and 16sts across left front shoulder and neckband side seam (32 sts in total).
Work 1 row.
Buttonhole row: K18, ** YRN, K2tog, K4*, rep from ** to * and work to the end.
Next row: work to end.
Cast off loosely.
Sew on buttons to correspond with buttonholes.

Making up

Join the left shoulder and neckband seam of the sweater, unless you have made a shoulder opening. Sew the sleeves evenly into the armholes (see page 52). Join the side and sleeve seams using mattress stitch. Press all seams gently.

Congratulations

You've done it! Excellent!

RIBBING

If this is the first sweater you have made, start with the back. It will be good practice as there is only minimal shaping, so by the time you get to the sleeves you will be able to cope better! The ribbing shown is known as K1, P1 rib. An alternative is K2, P2 rib, which produces a chunkier effect.

The completed ribbing, showing increases spaced evenly along the last row.

1 Knit the first stitch.

2 Purl the second stitch.

3 Repeat steps 1 and 2 to the end of the row.

RIB INCREASE

Although the ribbing is elastic, it is often necessary to increase the number of stitches across its width to give the body of the garment extra fullness. This is usually done on the last row of the rib, working the rest of the ribbing as normal.

1 Work in rib to where the increase is needed.

2 Pick up the loop between the stitches and place on the left needle.

3 Insert the needle in the back of the loop...

4 ...and knit it as a stitch.

The finished increase, which is also known as make one (M1)

45

SHAPING

The back of the sweater is shaped very simply by casting off at the armholes and working straight until the required length is reached. The centre stitches are cast off and two rows are worked on each shoulder section.

The front of the sweater is a little more complicated as it must also be shaped at the neck. This is done by dividing the stitches into sections, then working on one section at a time.

FRONT NECK SHAPING

The left side is worked first, then cast off. Rejoin the yarn to the stitches for the right front and complete, following the instructions given. The centre stitches are placed on a stitch holder, then taken off the holder and worked to complete the neckband. This helps to give a neat finish to the front of the sweater.

1 Work across the stitches for the first shoulder section.

2 Place the remaining stitches on a holder. Turn and complete the first shoulder section.

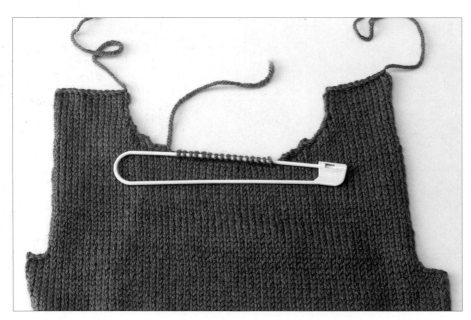

The sweater front, showing the armhole shaping and both shoulder sections completed, with the centre neck stitches on a stitch holder.

INCREASES

Increasing means adding stitches to make your work wider, therefore changing its shape. This is the most common type of increase, also known as M1.

1 Insert the needle in the first stitch and knit in the usual way...

2 ...but do not take the stitch off the needle.

3 Insert the needle in the back of the same stitch...

4 ...bring the yarn forward between the needles...

5 ...and knit the stitch, taking it off the needle.

6 Knit the next stitch, and carry on working...

7 ...so the extra stitch is incorporated in your work.

INCREASING PURLWISE

Increases must be made evenly on both sides of the sleeve. Some instructions show increases at both ends of the knit row. I prefer to increase at the beginning of alternate rows; first on the knit row, then on the purl row that follows.

To increase purlwise i.e. on the purl row, you must purl the first stitch, and purl into the back, then the front of the next stitch.

For an invisible increase purlwise, push the right needle, from the back to the front, into the stitch on the left needle but one row down. Purl this stitch and the next.

For sleeves, single stitches are added to the end of rows at regular intervals so the shape gradually widens.

INCREASE BETWEEN STITCHES (MAKE ONE)

This stitch can also be used in the middle or at the end of a row. It does not spoil the evenness of the knitted piece, but remember to work into the back of the stitch. If you forget to do this, a little hole will appear in your work, and this is both untidy and unattractive.

1 Pick up the loop between the stitch just worked and the next.

2 Transfer the loop to the left needle.

3 Insert the right needle into the back of the loop.

4 Yarn over...

5 ...and knit the stitch...

6 ...taking it off the needle, then work to the end of the row.

INVISIBLE INCREASE

This useful increase is 'invisible' – that is, it is difficult to see when the work is finished. It can be used at the end or in the middle of a row. Increases are shown on the knit row; for purl row increases see the instructions on page 47.

1 Push the right needle into the stitch on the left needle but one row down.

2 Knit the stitch in the usual way...

3 ...pulling the right needle through so that your work looks like this.

4 Knit the next stitch.

DECREASES

Decreasing is used to shape your work, by reducing the width of the knitted piece. In general, decreases should follow the line of the knitting, which means that decreases at the beginning of a row should slant to the left and decreases at the end should slant to the right. The slip stitch decrease shown here is the simplest and neatest way to decrease at the beginning of a knit row.

1 Push the right needle into the first stitch...

2 ...and slip it off without knitting it (known as sl1).

3 Knit the next stitch in the normal way...

4 ...and take it off the needle.

5 Push the needle into the slipped stitch...

6 ...and lift it over the knitted stitch (psso).

The finished decrease, shown worked on alternate rows of a sample of stockinette stitch.

Note
If you are working a piece of knitting that needs to be decreased at both edges, you can do this by working the slip stitch decrease at the beginning of the row and working two stitches together at the end. I prefer to increase at the beginning of each row as I find it helps me to get into a rhythm. The method I use for working decreases on a purl row of stockinette stitch is shown on page 50.

DECREASING PURLWISE

Working two stitches as though they were one is the simplest way to decrease. This is done on the wrong side of the work (the purl row) for a left slant.

1 Slip the right needle into the front of the first two stitches (sl2p).

2 Bring the yarn forward...

3 ...and purl both stitches together.

4 Slip both the stitches...

5 ...off the needle.

6 And purl the next stitch in the normal way.

The purlwise decreases shown on the right side of stockinette stitch.

Note

These decreases give a really neat edge that is ideal for shaping the neckline, armholes and sleeves of a sweater. They also give a clean, straight line up a raglan seam that is perfect for a garment in fine yarn. They are also useful for shaping the side seam of a sweater into a waistline, or to produce neat decreases on the back seam of a hat.

NECKBAND

Join the shoulder seam with a neat back stitch before you pick up the stitches to work the neckband. Use pins to divide the neck edge into equal sections and work with the right side facing. The cast-off stitches and decreases that shape the neck can leave an uneven edge, so follow the shape of the curve, one stitch in. This will cover up the uneven edge and help you to achieve a neat neckband.

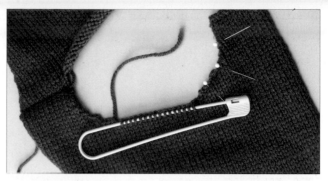

Place pins evenly round the curve

1 Push the needle in, one stitch from the edge. Take a length of yarn from the ball and wrap it round...

2 ...then use the point of the needle to pull the yarn through to the right side of the work.

3 Push the point of the needle into your work...

4 ...wrap the yarn round the needle...

6 ...and pull it through again as in step 2.

7 Carry on in this way all round the neck...

8 ...following the curve of the neck but one row in.

9 At the centre of the neck, knit across the stitches on the holder.

10 Pick up the stitches evenly from the right side of the neck edge.

All the stitches have been picked up across the front of the sweater.

THE BACK NECK

When you have finished picking up the stitches across the front neck, pick up the stitches evenly across the back neck so that all your stitches are on one needle.

You are now ready to work the neckband. You will find it easier to do this if you use needles that are long enough to hold all the stitches without crowding them too closely together.

The stitches have been picked up evenly across the back neck.

1 Start to work the neckband in K1, P1 rib.

2 Work in rows across all the stitches on the needle until the required length has been reached.

FINISHING THE NECKBAND

To cast off or bind off the neckband in rib, knit the first stitch and purl the second. Use the left needle to lift the knit stitch over the purl stitch. Knit the next stitch and lift the purl stitch over. Purl the next stitch and lift the knit stitch over. Repeat until all the stitches have been cast off.

Detail of neckband worked in K1, P1 rib and cast off in rib.

Casting off loosely using K1, P1 rib.

BUTTONHOLES

For a baby's sweater, you will need only a small buttonhole, which is very simple to make. Work to where you want the buttonhole but, instead of working the next stitch, take your yarn round the needle. This makes a hole and leaves a loop of yarn over the top of the needle. Knit the next two stitches together. When you work the next row, work a stitch into the loop above the new buttonhole.

To make a larger buttonhole suitable for chunkier garments, see the instructions on page 67.

1 Knit two stitches, yarn round the needle (YRN).

2 Insert the right needle into the next two stitches.

3 Knit both the stitches together.

4 Knit the next stitch...

5 ...and continue to the end of the row leaving a neat buttonhole.

Detail of the finished button band and buttons

53

MAKING UP SLEEVES

The look of your garment can be ruined if the sleeves are not sewn in neatly, but the steps here will help you to achieve a perfect result.

The underarm seam can be joined with back stitch or mattress stitch (see pages 32–33). I prefer mattress stitch, which is worked from the front so it is easier to match the stitches up row by row. After a little practice you will find it very easy.

Press the sleeves before you begin, and join the armhole edges of your work first. Use a needle with a large eye, and fasten the yarn to your work by oversewing a few stitches.

The completed sleeve, showing increases and decreases.

1 Using contrasting yarn, mark the centre sleeve to match it with the shoulder seam. Pass the yarn across...

2 ...to join the underarm points of the sleeve and the body piece.

3 Pull the edges together to join them.

4 Take the yarn back to the opposite edge and pick up the next stitch.

5 Take the needle and yarn back across to pick up the next stitch...

6 ...and pull gently to close the stitches.

7 Continue in the same way, pulling the stitches as you go...

8 ...to produce a seam that is almost invisible.

SEWING UP THE SEAMS

1 Take the yarn across at the lower edge of the rib to join the body pieces.

2 Take it back across to the right and match up with a stitch on the left.

3 Repeat the process one row up, matching stitch for stitch.

4 Continue to the top of the rib, then pull the yarn to join the two sides.

5 Turn the needle up and insert it between the first and second stitches of the first stockinette stitch row.

6 Repeat the procedure to join the side seam as far as the armhole. Join the other side seam.

7 Join the sleeve rib following steps 1–4, then take the yarn across ready to join the seam.

8 Follow the line of increases making sure that they match. Pull the yarn gently to close the seam.

9 Continue to match the stitches up the seam. Take care not to pull the yarn too tightly or the seam may pucker.

10 Join the seam to the armhole. Fasten off and join the other sleeve seam.

Mattress stitch makes a very neat, almost invisible seam.

Ringing the changes

The appearance of your garment can be changed easily by substituting different edgings. Moss stitch and rolled edgings are among the most useful, and a basic garment can be given a very different look simply by changing the edging used for the lower edge, cuffs and neckband – see the little sweaters on page 59.

Moss stitch gives a neat, firm and very pretty edge that is particularly effective on sweaters for babies. Rolled edging is looser and less structured, and is particularly good for casual sweaters.

Rolled edge

This edging is really easy: all you do is cast on and work in stockinette stitch. The edges will roll upwards automatically to produce the effect. For rolled edges on the basic sweater, cast on with size 3.25 (US size 3) needles and work 6 rows. Change to 4mm needles (US size 6) and continue. The edges of your work will curl naturally. Press lightly before making up.

Note: make sure you use 'invisible' increases (see page 48 for method) for a garment with a rolled edge.

Moss stitch

There are two different ways to work moss stitch, depending on the number of stitches in the row. For an odd number of stitches, the method is the same every row:
Patt row: *K1, P1, rep from * to the end of the row.

If you have an even number of stitches, moss stitch is worked over two rows:
Row 1: *K1, P1, rep from * to the end of the row.
Row 2: *P1, K1, rep from * to the end of the row.

Ringing the changes

These appealing sweaters show how a few changes can make the basic design look very different. In each case, the stripes were produced by joining in a different yarn every six rows. The multi-striped sweater was worked in oddments of Rowan Felted Tweed left over from the cushion and pram cover projects. The knobbly moss stitch edging used in place of rib on this sweater was inspired by the flecks in the yarn. If you are using up scraps of yarn, remember that they must be the same thickness, and check your tension or gauge carefully.

Adding motifs

Another way to add interest and individuality to a sweater is by adding a motif. You can work motifs into a garment, but it can be fiddly, so the easiest way is by Swiss Darning or duplicate stitch (see page 60). This wonderfully versatile technique involves embroidering over the top of the worked stitches and was originally developed to renovate old or worn knitwear. Today it is used to add interest to any garment. Use a tapestry needle to avoid splitting the yarn.

The most successful designs use yarn of a similar thickness over a light background, as a dark background can be hard to cover. Do not try anything too complicated as the impact will be lost. Simple shapes work best, like the cherry design here which was based on a cross stitch pattern. Size matters: decide where you want to place the design and make sure there is enough room. To plan your own design use squared or graph paper: each square represents a stitch.

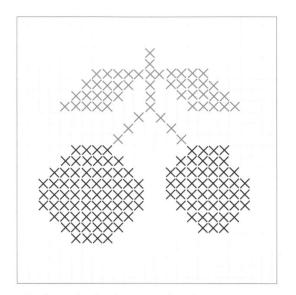

The design for the cherry motif on the sweater shown opposite. Each square represents a stitch.

Plan your design on graph paper using coloured pencils or felt-tipped pens. Keep the designs simple for maximum effect.

Magical Motifs

These plain sweaters were transformed by the addition of simple motifs. Design your own motif for the apple of your eye, but keep it simple. The design of Strawberries and Cream was inspired by warm summer days. Cheerful Cherries has a moss stitch edging. You will find matching hats for both these designs on page 77. Happy Heart has a rolled edging, and the motif is worked in mohair yarn to give a contrasting texture – see page 60 for method.

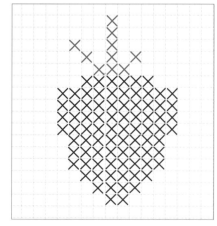

The chart for the strawberry design sweater.
The chart for the cherry motif is opposite.

STITCHING MOTIFS

This design is extremely useful and very easy to complete. I chose a mohair yarn to add interest to the front of a child's sweater. The hairs of mohair may drag as you sew: a good tip is to run it gently over a wax candle. This flattens the hair and makes it easier to use.

Before you begin, mark the centre of the area where the motif is to go with pins. This will be the centre point of the motif. Thread a tapestry needle with contrasting yarn and secure it to the wrong side of your work at the base of the design, which is where you will start to embroider. Bring the yarn through, take it up to the right and lay it over the first stitch as shown – see steps 1–3. Take care not to pull the yarn too tightly or your work will pucker.

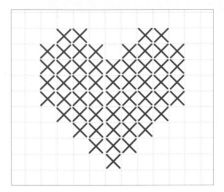

The chart for the heart motif

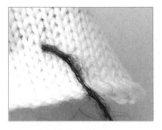

1 Secure the yarn and bring it through to the front of your work.

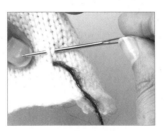

2 Insert the needle from right to left behind the stitch above...

3 ...and pull the yarn through to the left.

4 Take the needle through the base of the first stitch and back up to the front.

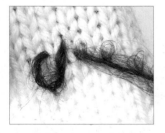

5 Come out level with the top of the first stitch, but one stitch to the right.

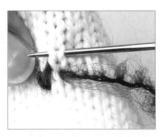

6 Work the next stitch from right to left as shown in steps 2–3.

7 Work in the same way until you reach the end of the second chart row.

8 Take the yarn up a row and one stitch to the left.

9 ...and cover the stitches in the same way.

10 Continue to work the block in vertical lines.

11 Secure yarn by weaving it in and out on the back.

The finished motif

POCKET-SIZED MOTIFS

Adding an embroidered pocket is another easy way to customise a plain sweater. For a pocket suitable for the basic sweater design, cast on 25 stitches and work 20 rows in stockinette stitch. Work 6 rows of K1, P1 rib and cast off. For a larger pocket, cast on more stitches. Mark the centre point of the pocket with pins before starting to embroider the design, and make sure there is room for it.

In general, it is best to work motifs from side to side, but on this anchor design a vertical line cannot be avoided. Begin at the bottom of the line by bringing the needle up through the base of the stitch.

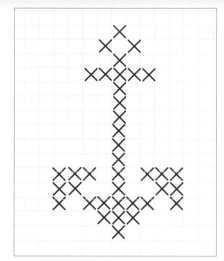

Anchor
This bold, simple anchor was inspired by a design on an old sampler. It can be used to brighten up a beanie hat, the front of a sweater or to trim a pocket.

1 Mark the centre of the pocket with pins. Work the first stitch.

2 Build up the motif one stitch at a time. Try to work horizontal lines as it is much flatter and neater.

3 Insert the needle behind the base of the stitch above...

4 ...back down into the base of the first stitch, then up again...

5 ...to work the vertical section of the design.

This anchor would also look effective used on the pram cover on page 36.

SEWING ON A POCKET

Mark out the position of the pocket with pins, using the lines of the work as a guide to make sure that it is straight. Pin the pocket in place. Secure the yarn to your work and sew the pocket on the front using slip stitch. Sew one side of the pocket in place first, then sew the bottom, easing into place if necessary.

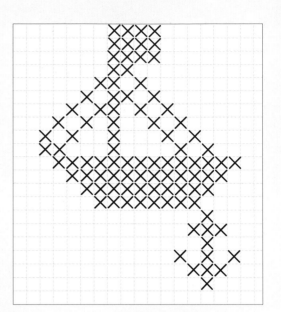

This design can be worked in different colours

1 Mark the position of the pocket with pins and pin it into place.

2 Start at the corner of the pocket and catch into position.

3 Take the yarn across and pick up the first stitch from the pocket.

4 Sew the first side in place, matching the stitches row for row.

5 Return to the lower edge and begin to sew the bottom of the pocket.

6 Oversew carefully, matching the stitches.

7 Finish the bottom edge of the pocket before sewing up the other side.

The finished pocket

A different effect
Try working the same motif in different shades of yarn.

The finished pocket
*Why not try ringing the changes by making two pockets –
one for each little hand? Or sew a smaller pocket higher
up on the sweater to make a safe place to keep a tiny toy.*

Classic Cardies

This loose, easy-living cardigan fits most sizes. Wear it over a T-shirt in summer or over a fine sweater in winter. The yarn used, Rowan Summer Tweed, is a delicious combination of silk and cotton with a lovely texture that is ideal for garter stitch. This yarn comes in hanks, so wind it into balls before you begin to knit. The design is truly one for all seasons: the same instructions can also be used to make a warm cardigan in chunky woollen yarn to ward off winter chills, with a simple collar added to keep out the wind (see page 70). Garter stitch has a springy texture that will be flattened by pressing, so your work should only be blocked – see page 15.

Summer Special

Back

Using 4.5mm (US 7) needles, cast on 104 sts and work 6 rows garter st.
Change to 5 mm (US 8) needles and begin the shaping.
Next row (dec): K1, K2tog, K to the last 3 sts, K2tog, K1.
Cont in garter st, dec as before on every 6th row (4 times), then every 10th row (3 times). There should be 88 sts on the needle.
Cont in garter st until your work measures 14in (36cm).
Next row: (armhole shaping) cast off 6 sts at the beg of the next 2 rows. Cont until work measures 10in (25.5cm) from armhole or 24in (61cm) from lower edge. Cast off.

Left Front

Using 4.5mm (US 7) needles, cast on 52 sts and work 6 rows in garter st.
Change to 5 mm (US 8) needles and work exactly as for the corresponding half of the back, dec and placing the armhole on the left side only. When your work measures 20in (51cm) from the lower edge, with the WS of the work facing, start to shape the neck.
Neck shaping: cast off 10 sts, work to end of row.
Knit 1 row.
Next row: cast off 2 sts, work to end.
Knit 1 row.
Next row: dec 1 st at neck edge, work to end of row (25 sts).
Work straight until front measures 24in (61cm).
Cast off.
Use lengths of contrasting yarn to mark buttonholes 1in (2.5cm) down from neck and at intervals of roughly 3in (7.5cm) – six buttonholes in total.

You will need

Rowan Summer Tweed (50g balls): 6 hanks Oats (508)

4.5mm (US 7) and 5mm (US 8) needles

Tapestry needle for sewing up

6 buttons

Glass-headed pins

Tape measure

Small amount of matching thread to sew on buttons

Tension (gauge): 19 sts and 30 rows to 4in (10cm) measured over garter st

Measurements: to fit bust size 34–40in (86–104); centre back length 23in (58cm)

Note
To help to keep my place in a pattern, I find it useful to place a coloured repositionable note under the relevant line, moving it as necessary.

The finished cardigan

The yarn used for this flattering cardigan is made from a mixture of 70% silk and 30% cotton. It has a wonderful texture, washes beautifully and should last for years. The sleeve cuffs can be turned back 5cm (2in) for a different effect.

Right Front

Using 4.5mm (US 7) needles cast on 52 sts and work as for left front, reversing shapings and working buttonholes as below, 3 sts in from the front edge to correspond with the position of the thread markers.

Buttonhole row 1: K 3 sts, cast off 2 sts. Work to end.

Buttonhole row 2: K to last 3 sts, make 2 sts to replace cast-off sts – see method on page 67.

Sleeves (both alike)

Using 4.5mm (US 7) needles cast on 40 sts and work 6 rows in garter st.

Change to 5mm (US 8) needles and inc 1st at each end of every 4th row (8 times).

Inc 1st at each end of every 6th row until there are 70 sts on the needle.

Work straight in garter st until work measures 50cm (19½in). Cast off.

Making up

Block the pieces and leave to dry thoroughly. Join the shoulder seams by oversewing, matching the ridges of the knitting. Fold the sleeve in half and mark with contrasting thread (see photograph below). Sew in the sleeves. Join the side and sleeve seams.

Shape the armhole by casting off 6 stitches.

Cast off and decrease to shape the neck edge.

Mark the centre of the sleeve top to line it up with the shoulder seam.

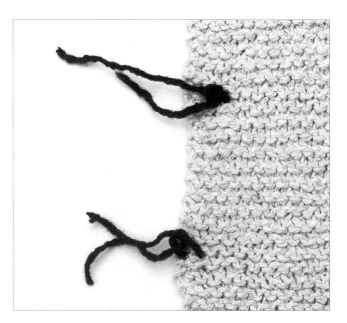

Mark the position of the buttonholes on the left front.

LARGER BUTTONHOLES

These are made in a slightly different way from the buttonholes used for the baby's sweater (see page 53).

If you have chosen very large buttons, you may need to cast off more stitches for each buttonhole. Remember that buttonholes can become loose with wear so do not be tempted to be over-generous when making them. The technique is shown on a stockinette stitch sample for clarity.

1 Work to the buttonhole position. Cast off the next stitch, using the left needle to pick up the previous stitch.

2 Lift it over the last stitch knitted.

3 Cast off the next stitch, then work to the end of the row. Turn your work ready for the next row.

4 Work up to the buttonhole, then loop the yarn round the right needle.

5 Pull gently to close the loop on the needle.

6 Make another loop in the same way. Work to the end of the row.

7 Work back across the row, incorporating the 'loop' cast-on stitches into your work. Work straight until you reach the position of the next buttonhole.

FLAT SEAMS

These are done with the right side of the work facing. They give a very neat finish without bulk, and the ridges on the garter stitch make it particularly easy to do.

1 Take the yarn across from the left edge to the right edge and pull it gently to close.

2 Pick up one little knot on the edge from the right side...

3 ...and take the yarn across to pick up the corresponding knot on the other side.

4 Every few stitches, draw the thread up gently to close the seam.

SEWING ON BUTTONS

If your yarn is thick or textured, it will not be ideal for sewing on buttons.
The best option is to use strong thread in a shade similar to the yarn.

1 Secure the thread with several oversewn stitches and sew on the button.

2 Take the thread through the button two or three times to fasten it securely. Finish by oversewing several stitches on the wrong side. Cut off the thread.

Note
Sew a spare button down the side seam of the finished cardigan in case one is lost.

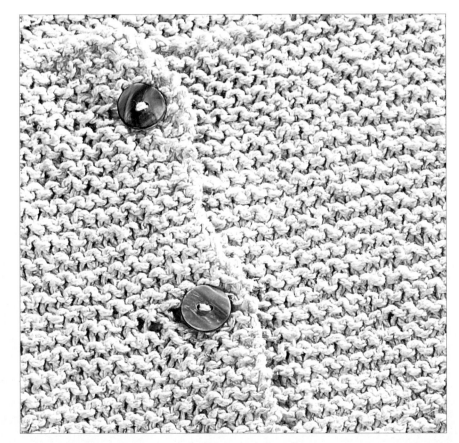

Choosing your buttons with care will make a big difference to your finished cardigan

Winter Warmer

This wonderfully cosy chunky cardigan is made using the same instructions as the summer cardigan on page 64 but with different yarn. I fell in love with the yarn – it was so bright and cheery that I thoroughly enjoyed making it. I added an extra buttonhole to cope with the thickness of the yarn, and a simple collar (see below).

Back, Fronts and Sleeves

Work exactly as for *Summer Special* (see page 64) but measure out and make one extra buttonhole on the right front.

Collar

Using 5mm (US 8) needles cast on 58 sts and work in garter st until work measures 7in (18cm). Cast off loosely.

Making up

Complete as for *Summer Special* (see page 66). Oversew the collar evenly in place, starting 1in (25mm) in from the front edge.

Detail of collar

You will need

Rowanspun Chunky (100g hanks): 10 hanks Hearty (992)

4.5mm (US 7) and 5mm (US 8) needles

7 buttons

Tapestry needle for sewing up

Tape measure

Glass-headed pins

Small amount of matching thread to sew on buttons

Tension (gauge): 14 sts and 16 rows to 4in (10cm) measured over garter st

Measurements: to fit up to bust size 42in (106cm). Centre back length: 24in (61cm)

1 Stretch the collar evenly round the neck using thread markers.

2 Thread the needle and secure the yarn with a few stitches.

3 Oversew in place, matching the thread markers. Fasten off.

The finished Chunky jacket

*This loose, chunky jacket looks great whatever your size, and
the sleeves can be turned back for a different look.*

Happy Hats

Hats are easy and fast to make, and can be made to look very different by adding stripes, tassels, pompoms or other embellishments. It is not difficult to make up your own designs: for an adult, a hat should be about 21½in (54.5cm) round the lower edge and 7in (18cm) from lower edge to crown. For a child the measurement should be about 19½in (50cm) round the lower edge and 6¼in (16cm) to the crown. The smallest baby size should measure about 14in (36cm) round the lower edge and 5½in (14cm) to the crown.

The hats shown mostly involve putting stitches on your needle and working rows straight, then decreasing to shape the top or crown. The easiest and quickest hat, made from chunky garter stitch hat in shades of brown, took about an hour. It couldn't be easier! Instructions are on page 75.

Almost as easy was the mushroom-coloured hat with a ribbed edge (centre left on the photograph opposite). This was made in reversed stockinette stitch, which means that the wrong (ridged) side of stockinette stitch is used for the outside of the hat. The knitted fabric looks rather like garter stitch, but is not as thick. Both hats fit adults, and there's no need to press them. Instructions are below.

Polar Hat

Cast on 71 sts and work 1½in (4cm) K1, P1 rib, ending with a RS row so the reverse of the stockinette stitch is on the outside of the hat.
Work 20 rows SS.
Next row (crown shaping): K2 *K2tog, K4, rep from * to last 3 sts, K2tog (59 sts).
P 1 row.
Next row: K2 *K2tog, K2, rep from * to last st, K1 (45 sts).
Work 3 rows SS.
Next row: K2 *K2tog, K1, rep from * to last st, K1 (31 sts).
P 1 row.
Next row: K2tog across row, K1 (16 sts on needle).
P 1 row.
Next row: K2tog across row.
Next row: K2tog across row.

Making up

Break off yarn and thread end on a tapestry needle. Thread through sts and pull gently to close. Join back seam. Fasten off.

You will need

Rowan Polar: 1 x 100g ball Stony (640)

8mm (US 11) needles

Tapestry needle for sewing up

Tape measure

Glass-headed pins

Tension (gauge): 12 sts and 16 rows to 4in (10cm)

Measurements: to fit adult size

A selection of hats in all types of yarn

Basic Beanie

With 3.25mm (US 3) needles and Mariner cast on 96 (116,128) sts and work 4 rows garter st.

Change to 4mm (US 6) needles and work 32 (36,44) rows.

Next row (crown shaping): K1 * K3tog, K14 (16,18), rep from * to last st, K1. 84 (104,116) sts.

Work 1 (1,3) rows.

Next row: K1 * K3tog, K12 (14, 16) sts, rep from * to last st, K1.

Work 1 (1,3) rows.

Next row: K1 * K3tog, K10 (12, 14) sts, rep from * to last st, K1.

Work 1 (1,1) row.

Cont to dec in this way, i.e. working two fewer sts between decs on subsequent alt rows, until 20 sts rem.

Work 1 row.

Next row: K1 (K2tog) across row (11 sts).

Break off yarn. Thread the end of the yarn through all sts and sew up. At the top of the crown, oversew a few sts to finish. Pin and sew the back seam, matching the ridges of the garter st.

You will need

Jaeger Matchmaker Merino Double Knitting (50g balls): 1 (1, 2) balls of Mariner (629)

3.25mm (US 3) and 4mm (US 6) needles

Tapestry needle for sewing up

Tape measure

Glass-headed pins

Tension (gauge): 22 sts and 30 rows to 4in (10cm) measured over SS on 4mm (US 6) needles

Measurements: first baby size is given; child and adult sizes follow in brackets

Note

These practical beanie hats are suitable for all the family, and garter stitch gives them a wonderful texture. The crown shaping is done in sections, with each decrease worked on top of the decrease on the previous row. This gives a very neat finish to the hat.

Basic beanie hats

A variation to match the striped scarf shown on page 23 can be made by following the basic beanie hat instructions opposite but working in a sequence of 6 rows per stripe.

74

FINISHING OFF

1 Cast on and work straight following pattern.

2 Work the decreases until 11 sts remain.

3 Break off the yarn and thread through...

4 ...the stitches from the needle.

5 Draw the yarn through all the stitches.

6 Pull gently to close.

7 Fasten off at the top of the crown.

8 Pin and oversew the back seam, matching the ridges of the garter stitch.

Chunky Hat

Cast on 24 sts and K 12 rows garter st.
Next row (crown shaping): K2tog across the row (12 sts).
Next row: (K2tog) 6 times (6 sts).
Break off the yarn and complete as for the Polar Hat on page 72.

You will need

Rowan Biggy Print: 1 x 100g ball Glum (244)

20mm (US 36) needles

Tapestry needle for sewing up

Tension (gauge): 5½ sts and 7 rows to 4in (10cm)

Measurements: to fit adult size

The finished hat

Shapely Stockinette

This little hat with a contrasting rolled edge can also be worked completely plain; in jaunty stripes; without a motif or with a different motif; with ribbing or moss stitch instead of a rolled edge; topped with a tassel or a pompom, or made to look like your favourite fruit. The basic instructions are here – what you make of them is up to you!

With 3.25mm (US 3) needles and Mariner cast on 96 (116, 128) sts and work 6 rows SS (1 row K, 1 row P) for the rolled edging. Break off yarn and join in Light Natural.

Change to 4mm (US 6) needles and work 28 (32, 40) rows.

Next row (crown shaping): K1 * K3tog, K14 (16, 18), rep from * to last st, K1 – 84 (104, 116) sts.

Work 1 (1, 3) rows.

Next row: K1 * K3tog, K12 (14,16), rep from * to last st, K1.

Work 1 (1, 3) rows.

Next row: K1 * K3tog, K10 (12, 14), rep from * to last st, K1.

Work 1 row.

Next and foll alt rows: cont to dec in this way, i.e. working two fewer sts between decs, until 20 sts rem.

Work 1 row.

Next row: K1 (K2tog) across row (11 sts). Break off yarn. Thread end of yarn through all sts and draw together. Join back seam.

You will need

Jaeger Matchmaker Merino Double Knitting (50g balls): 1 ball Light Natural (663)

Small amount of the same yarn in Mariner (629) for the rolled edging

3.25mm (US 3) and 4mm (US 6) needles

Tapestry needle for sewing up

Tape measure

Glass-headed pins

Tension (gauge): 22 sts and 30 rows to 4in (10cm) measured over SS on 4mm (US 6) needles

Measurements: first baby size is given; child and adult sizes follow in brackets

This simple stockinette stitch beanie in cream-coloured yarn was made special by adding a contrasting rolled edge and an anchor motif – see page 61. The contrast trim and anchor were added using a small amount of the same yarn in Mariner (669).

Fantastic Fruit

These fun hats complement the strawberry and cherry sweaters on page 59. Make a basic beanie hat with a rolled edge and sew a knitted 'stalk' to the crown. For the strawberry hat, add embroidered 'pips' (see below). For the cherry hat, add knitted leaves (see below) and attach to the hat as shown. Making the leaves will test your invisible increase skills (see page 48).

Strawberry Fair

Hat: using Rosy, work as for the Basic Beanie (see page 74).

Stalk: using Loden and 3.25mm (US 3) needles cast on 8 sts and K 1 row. Cast off.

Making up: fold in half, sew tog and attach to top of hat. Fasten off inside.

Pips: using Loden, darn in the 'pips' at random intervals, making each pip two stitches high.

You will need

Jaeger Matchmaker Merino DK (50g balls): 1 ball Rosy (870). Small amount of the same yarn in Loden (730) for stalk and embroidery

3.25mm (US 3) and 4mm (US 6) needles

Tapestry needle

Adding the pips

Work the pips as little inverted 'V' shapes, two stitches high.

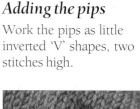

Cherry Ripe

Hat: using Cherry, work as for the Basic Beanie (see page 74).

Stalk: work as for Strawberry Fair.

Leaves (two alike): Using 3.25mm (US 3) needles, cast on 3 sts and work 2 rows SS.

Next row: K1, M1, K1, M1, K1 (5 sts).

Next row: P.

Next row: K1, M1, K3, M1, K1 (7 sts). P 1 row.

Next row: K1, M1, K5, M1, K1 (9 sts).

Beg with P, SS 4 rows.

Making up: Break off yarn, thread through sts. Attach leaves to hat as shown in steps (see right). Catch stitch points to hat.

You will need

Jaeger Matchmaker Merino DK: 1 x 50g ball Cherry (656). Scrap of the same yarn in Loden (730) for stalk and leaves

3.25mm (US 3) and 4mm (US 6) needles

1 Thread yarn through the wide end of the leaf...

2 ...and gather it as you attach it by the stalk.

3 Fasten off neatly with a few stitches.

Stunning Squares

This hat based on a simple square is an ideal project for a beginner as there is no shaping to worry about. The interesting shape of the hat emerges when yarn plaits, which are sewn to the corners of the hat, are tied through a yarn loop in the centre of the crown.

Instructions are given in three sizes: for the first baby size, a child and adult. The smallest size is given first with the different size variations in brackets.

Front and back (both alike)

Using 3.25mm (US 3) needles cast on 50 (55, 57) sts and work 1½in (4cm) K1, P1, rib.
Change to 4mm (US 6) needles and work in SS for 38 (48, 62) rows.
Cast off. Make another piece the same.

Making up

Press both pieces. Pin together with the rib at the lower edge. Sew up using mattress stitch round the three stockinette stitch edges.

You will need

Jaeger Matchmaker Merino DK (50g balls): 1 (2, 2) balls Mariner (629)

3.25mm (US 3) and 4mm (US 6) needles

Tapestry needle for sewing up

Tape measure

Glass-headed pins

Iron and padded surface

Tension (gauge): 22 sts and 30 rows to 4in (10cm) over SS on 4mm (US 6) needles

Measurements: to fit baby (child, adult)

MAKING THE LOOP AND TIES

1 Sew a yarn loop in the centre of the crown.

2 Loop twice round your finger...

3 ... and blanket stitch neatly round the loop.

4 Finish the blanket stitch and fasten off.

5 Make two plaits, each with six lengths of yarn 14in (36cm) long. Tie off the ends, attach a plait to each corner of the hat, then thread through the loop.

6 Pull the plait to draw the corners of the hat in and tie in a bow at the centre of the crown.

This innovative little hat is made in exactly the same way as the basic hat. It gets its shape from yarn plaits tied through a loop, which give it a fun look as well as adding shape.

Striped Hat

Following the basic instructions, work 1½in (4cm) K1, P1 rib.
Join in Light Natural and knit 6 rows, then change to Mariner and work 6 rows. Repeat until your work is the length required.
Cast off and finish as for the basic hat (see page 74).

You will need

Jaeger Matchmaker Merino DK (50g balls): 1 ball Mariner (629) and 1 ball Light Natural (663) for all sizes

Needles etc. as for basic hat

Note

When I knit in stripes, I break off the yarn instead of trying to carry it up the side of my work as I think it gives a neater finish. I use the ends to sew up the garment in stripe sequence.

Sailor stripes
This little hat with a jaunty nautical feel looks fantastic with a matching sweater (see page 1). Trim it with small tassels.

Perfectly Peruvian

This little hat in simple garter stitch is a weekend project and fun to make. Change the colours, make deeper stripes, add longer plaits to the ear flaps or even add a tassel to the crown. Above all, enjoy yourself!

The baby's version below needed only a small plait. For the child's version I made longer plaits using Berry, Toad and Charcoal plaited together – see opposite. The yarn used comes in hanks so you will be able to have fun winding it into balls!

You will need

Rowan Magpie Aran (100g hanks):

Baby hat: 1 hank Prance (697)

Child's striped hat: 1 hank each of Berry (684); Prance (697); Toad (694); Coffee Bean (685); Charcoal (635) and Raven (062)

Adult's striped hat: 1 hank each of Raven (062) and Berry (684) (*shown on page 73*)

Tension (gauge): 17 sts and 36 rows to 4in (10cm) measured over garter st

5mm (US 8) needles

Crochet hook

Glass-headed pins

Tape measure

Tapestry needle for sewing up

The baby's hat worked in the smallest size

Hat

Cast on 56 (84, 88) sts and K 30 (36, 48) rows.

Next row (crown shaping): *K4, K2tog, rep from * to end of row.
K 1 row.

Next row: *K2, K2tog, rep from * to end of row.

Adult size only: rep last 2 rows.
K 1 row.

Next row: *K1, K2tog, rep from * to end of row.

Adult size only: rep last 2 rows.
K1 row.

Next row: (K2tog) to end
K1 row.

Next row: (K2tog) to end
K1 row.

Break yarn, thread through rem sts and draw tog. Join back seam.

Ear flaps

Cast on 3 sts. K 2 rows.

Every foll row: inc 1st at the beg of the row until there are 16 (27, 29) sts on the needle.

Adult size only: work 2 more rows without shaping. Cast off.

Making up

Place the ear flaps ½in (1cm) in from the back seam and oversew to hat, matching the stitches. Cut lengths of yarn for the plaits and use a crochet hook to thread them through the ends of the ear flaps. Plait the lengths of yarn and tie off the ends.

Sew on the ear flaps neatly, matching the stitches.

MAKING THE PLAITS

1 Cut lengths of yarn and pull them through the ends of the ear flaps using a crochet hook...

2 ...leaving a loop...

3 ...to pull the yarn through.

4 Plait the lengths of the yarn.

5 Tie off using a double knot.

Note
The adult version of this hat can be seen on page 73.

The child's hat
The child's striped hat can be made using fewer colours. You will still need only one hank of each.

MAKING POMPOMS

Any hat can be made into a pompom hat! You can add one pompom or several, and tiny pompoms also make a fun decoration for the edge of a scarf. Why not add one to the lower edge of the earflaps on the Peruvian hat?

First, decide how large a pompom you need. As a guide, a circle 3in (7.5cm) in diameter with a 1¼in (3cm) inside circle makes a 3in (7.5cm) pompom. Cut two circles from firm card (cereal packets are ideal), then cut out smaller inner circles from the larger card circles. Place the templates together. Wind off a small amount of yarn, small enough to push through the centre hole. The more yarn you wind round your template, the fuller your pompom will be.

1 Cut out two templates from firm card. Wind off a small amount of yarn.

2 Hold one end of the yarn to the card and start winding the yarn round.

3 Carry on winding the yarn evenly and firmly around the card.

4 When the hole is nearly full, finish by threading the yarn on a needle.

5 Ease the point of a pair of scissors between the wound yarn and the card.

6 Start snipping through the wound yarn a few strands at a time.

7 Continue snipping round the template ...

8 ...until all the strands of yarn have been cut.

9 Loop a double length of yarn between the cards...

10 ...and tie the ends off tightly to secure them.

11 Carefully tear away the card circles.

12 Trim the pompom to a nice round shape.

Finished pompoms

Make as many pompoms as you need, in either one colour or several different colours. Multicoloured pompoms can be made by winding more than one colour round the template.

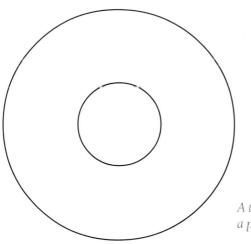

A template for a pompom

Note
Do not trim the length of yarn used to secure the pompom as this can be used to sew the pompom to your hat or garment.

This simple stockinette stitch hat has been given a jaunty pompom in yarn to match the rolled-edge trim.

Perfect Patterns

All-over designs can make a simple sweater look absolutely fabulous. Start by working mock cables that look almost as good as the real thing, then increase your skills by learning to cable stitches using a special cable needle (see pages 92–93).

Lace With a Twist

This sweater may look complicated, but is amazingly easy as it uses the mock cable Barley Twist pattern (see below and page 89). It was finished off with a lacy edging that is really easy to work and grows very quickly. It was devised by a friend, so I call it Diane's Border. I have included two alternative lace edgings, either of which you can substitute if you prefer (see pages 87–88).

Back

Using 3.25mm (US 3) needles cast on 122 sts.
Work in Barley Twist pattern, dec 1st at each end of every 4th row and *keeping the patt correct* (see note) until 112 sts rem.
Work 10 rows without shaping.
Next and every foll 6th row: inc 1 st at each end of row until there are 122 sts on needle.
Work 30 rows without shaping.
Armhole shaping: cast off 4 sts at beg of next 2 rows.
Next 12 rows: dec 1 st at each end of row (90 sts).
Next 2 alt rows: dec 1 st at each end of row (86 sts)*.
Cont in patt until work measures 16½in (42cm) from lower edge.
Cast off in patt.

Barley Twist pattern
Worked over 5 sts plus 2

Row 1: (wrong side) K2, P5

Row 2: P2, K2tog but do not slip the sts off the needle, knit into the first st of the K2tog again, K1, P2

Row 3: K2, P3, K2

Row 4: P2, K1, K2tog but do not slip the sts off the needle, K into the first st of the K2tog again, P2

You will need

Rowan Cotton Glace (50g balls): 6 balls of white

3.25mm (US 3) needles

Stitch holder

Tapestry needle for sewing up

Iron and padded surface

Tape measure

Glass-headed pins

Tension (gauge): 28 sts and 38 rows to 4in (10cm) measured over SS

Measurements: all round under arms without stretching 36in (91cm); sleeve length 19½in (49.5cm); centre back length (excluding trim) 16½in (42cm)

Trim: all round lower edge 37in (94cm); cuff about 8in (20cm); neck edge 35in (89cm)

Note
Keep the Barley Twist pattern correct as you decrease, remembering that it will not always be possible to twist the stitches as you decrease them. Do not worry when this happens: either knit or purl the stitch, then continue in pattern.

The finished sweater
The effect can be varied by choosing a
different lace edging. If you prefer a plainer
effect, a strip of moss stitch would make an
attractive alternative to lace.

Front

Work as for back until*
Work 1 row in patt.

Neck shaping: with RS facing patt 33 sts. Slip rem sts on to holder, turn and work on the 33 sts.

Next and foll 4 alt rows: cast off 2 sts at neck edge (23 sts rem).

Foll 9 alt rows: dec 1 st at neck edge (14 sts).

Work straight on these 14 sts until front measures the same as the back. Cast off in patt.

With RS facing rejoin yarn to rem sts. Cast off centre 20 sts, patt to end.

Complete the second side of the neck on these sts, reversing all shapings.

Sleeves

Using 3.25mm (US 3) needles cast on 50 sts. Work in patt, inc 1 st at each end of every 5th row until there are 100 sts on your needle.

Work 5 rows without shaping.

Next 2 rows (sleeve top): cast off 4 sts at the beg, work to end.

Next 11 rows: dec 1 st at each end of row (70 sts).

Next and foll 17 alt rows: dec 1 st at each end of row (36 sts).

Next 5 rows: dec 1 st at each end (26 sts).

Cast off in patt.

Making up

Do not press your work as this will flatten the texture. Block all the pieces and stretch them slightly. Spray lightly and leave to dry thoroughly.

Working the border

Choose a lace border pattern from the three included in this section. The garment shown as finished with Diane's Border (see pattern opposite). Using 3mm (US 2–3) needles, work a piece long enough for the lower edge of the sweater, stretching slightly, and finishing on the last row of the relevant border pattern. Do the same for each of the sleeves. Work another section of border for the neckline, noting that the finished border will stand up all round the neckline.

Sewing on the border

Stretch the border evenly and pin in place. Always join the border on a seam, as it will give a neater finish. Ease into place if necessary, especially round the neckline shaping. Slip stitch the edge of the border neatly in place, taking care not to pull the yarn too tightly as you sew.

Detail of finished sleeve trim

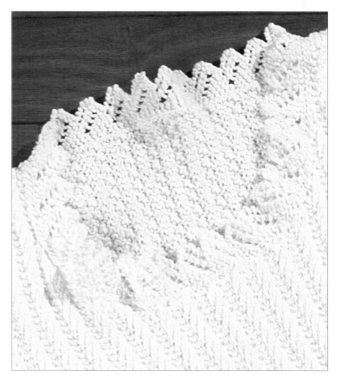

Detail of finished neckline

Lace edgings

Any of these edgings can be used to finish the sweater shown on page 85. The example shown features Diane's Border, which is far easier to work than it looks. Repeat the pattern rows for the border you have chosen until your work is long enough to fit round the relevant edge, slightly stretched. Cast off.

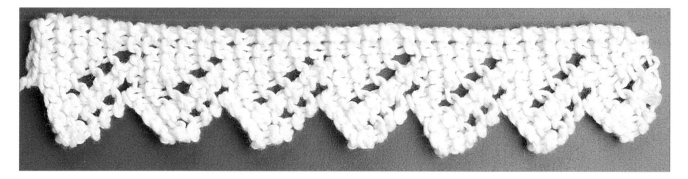

A sample section of Diane's Border

Diane's Border

Cast on 5 sts.
Row 1: K2, YO, K2tog, YO, K1.
Row 2: K.
Row 3: K3, YO, K2tog, YO, K1.
Row 4: K.
Row 5: K4, YO, K2tog, YO, K1.
Row 6: K.
Row 7: K5, YO, K2tog, YO, K1.
Row 8: K.
Row 9: K.
Row 10: cast off 4 sts, work to end.
Rep these rows until required length is reached, ending on a 10th row. Cast off. Sew to garment following instructions on page 86.

A sample section of Garter Wave edging

Garter Wave edging

Cast on 7 sts
Row 1: K2, YRN, K2tog, YRN, K to end
Row 2: K
Rows 3–15: rep rows 1 and 2, 6 more times.
Next row: rep row 1
Row 16: cast off 8 sts, K to end.
Rep these rows until the required length is reached, ending on a 16th row. Cast off and finish as for *Diane's Border*.

SIMPLE FILIGREE LACE

This open, lacy pattern is another attractive alternative trim. It is slightly more complicated than the others examples because it features a stitch known as YO2. This means that you must take the yarn over (or round) the needle twice before working the next stitch. You may also see this instruction written as YRN2 or YRN (twice).

    To work the pattern, cast on 6 stitches and repeat the four pattern rows to the length required. Cast off and follow the instructions on page 86 to sew on. See the steps below for hints on working row 1.

Cast on 6 stitches
Row 1: K1, K2tog, YO, K2, YO2, K1.
Row 2: K1, knit into the front, then the back of the YO2 from the row below, K2tog, YO, K3.
Row 3: K1, K2tog, YO, K5.
Row 4: cast off 2 sts, K2tog, YO, K3.

A sample section of simple filigree lace

Working row 1 of the pattern

1 K1, then K2 tog (row 1).

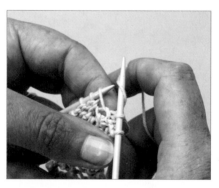

2 Yarn over the needle once as shown, then K2.

2 Yarn over the needle twice as shown, then K1.

Mock Cables

Mock cables are made without a cable needle. It is easier and quicker to work than cable and can look very similar. The process involves twisting stitches to make a textured design that appears to travel over the surface of the work. These instructions produce the cable-effect pattern used for *Lace with a Twist* (see page 84).

Detail of Barley Stitch mock cable

Barley Twist mock cable

This design is worked over 5 stitches plus 2 extra stitches

Row 1: (wrong side facing) K2, P5
Row 2: P2, K2tog but do not slip the sts off the needle, K into the first st of the K2tog again, K1, P2
Row 3: K2, P3, K2
Row 4: P2, K1, K2tog but do not slip the sts off the needle. K into the first st of the K2tog again, P2.

1 Row 4: P the first two stitches, then K1.

2 Knit 2 sts together...

3 ...but do not slip them off the left needle.

4 Insert the right needle into the first st of the K2tog again.

5 K into the st...

6 ..and slip it off the needle taking the K2 tog with it.

7 P the next two sts.

Country Cable

Since I designed and made this round-necked cardigan with moss stitch trim I have worn it constantly. The Aran Braid cable pattern I used may look complicated, but it is actually only four easy rows.

Back

With 3.25mm (US 3) needles cast on 122 sts and work 1¼in (3cm) moss st (see page 56). Change to 4mm (US 6) needles and work in cable patt:

Rows 1 and 3 (wrong side): *K2, P8, rep from * to end, K2.
Row 2: *P2, (C2B twice), rep from * to end, P2.
Row 4: *P2, K2, C2F, K2, rep from * to end, P2.
Rep these 4 rows until work measures 12in (30.5cm).
Next 2 rows (armhole shaping): cast off 4sts at the beg, work to end.
Next 16 rows: dec 1 st at the beg of row, work to end.*
Work without shaping to 21¼in (54cm). Cast off in patt.

Left front

With 3.25mm (US 3) needles cast on 62 sts and work as for half the back until your knitting measures 17½in (43cm).
Next row (shape front neck): with RS facing, cast off 4 sts at neck edge, work to end of row.
Next and foll rows: dec 1 st at neck edge until 31sts rem.
Work without shaping until front measures the same as the back.

Right front

Complete to match left front, reversing all shapings.

Sleeves (make 2 alike)

Using 3.25mm (US 3) needles cast on 72 sts. Work 1¼in (3cm) moss st. Change to 4mm (US 6) needles and work in pattern. *Keeping patt correct,* inc 1 st at each end of every 3rd row until there are 128 sts on the needle. Cont straight until work measures 19½in (50cm).
Next two rows: cast off 8 sts at beg of row.
Cast off rem sts.
Join shoulder seams using back stitch.

Front bands

Left band: using 3.25 (US 3) needles cast on 10 sts. Work in moss st until work measures 16½in (42cm). Stretch the band slightly up the front edge to check the length. Slip sts on to a holder. Using contrasting thread, mark the position for buttons 1¼in (3cm) from the bottom edge and 1½in (4cm) from the top edge. Space three more buttons evenly between.

Right (button) band: cast on 10 sts and work in moss st, placing buttonholes over sts 5 and 6 of the appropriate rows. When buttonholes have been worked cont in moss st for a further 1½in (4cm). End with the RS of the work facing, then work the neckband.

You will need

Rowan Felted Tweed (50g balls): 8 balls of Corn (136)

3.25mm (US 3) needles and dpn: 4mm (US 6) needles

6 buttons

Tapestry needle for sewing up

Small amount of matching thread to sew on buttons

Glass-headed pins

Tape measure

Tension (gauge): 23 sts and 30 rows to 4in (10cm) measured over stockinette stitch, not the Aran Braid cable pattern

Measurements: to fit bust size 34–36in (86–90cm) loosely.

Aran Braid Cable

Panel worked over 12 sts

Rows 1 and 3: *K2, P8, rep from * to end, K2.

Row 2: *P2, (C2B twice), rep from * to end, P2.

Row 4: *P2, K2, C2F, K2, rep from * to end, P2.

Note: row 1 is the wrong side

Neckband

Note: complete the two front bands before picking up the neckband.
Knit across the 10 sts of the button band. Pick up 24 sts evenly up the RS of the neck, 36 sts across the back neck and 24 sts down the left neck. Pick up the left band sts from the holder. Knit 1¼in (3cm) moss st, placing a buttonhole after ½in (1cm). Cast off loosely in moss st.

Making up

Block and press all pieces. The felted yarn will take quite a firm press and steam. Slip stitch the bands in place down the fronts. Fold the sleeves in half, lining up the centre with the shoulder seam, and sew into the armhole. Join the side and sleeve seams. Sew on the buttons.

Wearing

Put on your cardigan and admire the effect – you really have learned how to knit. Now go out and impress your friends!

The finished cardigan
This design is so comfortable it feels like an old friend. The yarn used washes beautifully and the colour shown seems to go with everything.

Note
You can substitute one of the cable stitches shown on pages 94–95 if you prefer. If you do, make sure that you check your tension (gauge) carefully.

CABLE STITCH

Cables are one of the most interesting stitches to work and have been used to great effect by designers. They look complicated but they are actually quite easy. The rope-like effect is achieved by using a short, double-pointed needle (dpn), which holds the cable stitches at the front or back while you work the stitches that are not being cabled.

To avoid stretched, baggy stitches, use a cable needle a size smaller.

CABLE FORWARD

The example shows a simple cable worked over six stitches. It forms a rope-like effect with all the crossings going the same way.

1 Cable 3 forward (C3F) Push the dpn into the first 3 sts of the cable.

2 Slide the sts off the knitting needle and on to the dpn.

3 Hold the dpn at the front of the work.

4 K the next 3 sts.

5 Now bring the sts on the dpn up...

6 ...and K the first st...

7 ...so your work looks like this...

8 K the rest of the sts.

9 Purl to the start of the next cable.

CABLE BACK

The procedure for cabling back is similar, but the stitches on the cable needle are held at the back of the work. Cable instructions use the abbreviation CB or CF with a number between. This is the number of stitches you should hold on a cable or double-pointed needle (dpn) at the front or back of your work. Knit the same number of stitches, then knit the stitches from the dpn to form the cable.

Cables are often worked on a background of reverse stockinette stitch to enhance their texture. The steps below show C3B (cable 3 back).

The stitches on the right have been cabled back and the stitches on the left are about to be cabled.

1 Slip the first 3 sts on to the dpn.

2 Hold the sts on the dpn at the back of the work.

3 K the first st from the left needle...

4 ..then K the rem sts.

5 K the first st from the dpn...

6 ...then the rest of the sts (C3B completed).

7 P to the start of the next cable.

WORKING THE FRONT BANDS AND NECKBAND

The bands for this cardigan are completed before you start to pick up the stitches round the neck. The final buttonhole is put into the neckband – refer to knitting instructions.

1 K across the front band, then insert your needle in the first stitch of the front of the cardigan...

2 ...and start to pick up the stitches round the neck.

Cable Variations

Any of the cable stitches on these pages could be substituted for the Aran Braid cable (see sample right) used to work *Country Cable* on page 90.

Cable patterns can be used on a wide variety of knitted items, either singly for effect or as an all-over fabric with reversed stockinette stitch between panels of cable.

Cables draw the work in widthwise but this varies according to the pattern, so make sure that you knit a tension (gauge) sample first.

The Aran Braid pattern used for the cardigan on page 90

Chain Cable

Panel worked over 12 stitches

Row 1: K2, P8, K2
Row 2: P2, C2B, C2F, P2
Row 3: as row 1
Row 4: P2, K8, P2
Row 5: as row 1
Row 6: P2, C2F, C2B, P2.
Row 7: as row 1
Row 8: P2, K8, P2

Note: the first row is the wrong side of the pattern.

Gull Stitch

Also known as Wishbone or Lobster Claw
Panel worked over 10 stitches.

Row 1: K2, P6, K2.
Row 2: P2, K2, sl2 wyib, K2, P2.
Row 3: K2, P2, sl2 wyif, P2, K2.
Row 4: P2, sl next 2 sts to dpn and hold at back, K1, K2 from dpn, sl next st to dpn and hold in front, K2, then K1 from dpn, P2.

Special abbreviations:
wyif: *with yarn held in front*
wyib: *with yarn held in back*
Note: the first row is the wrong side of the pattern.

Cable Braid

Panel worked over 14 stitches

Row 1: K2, P10, K2.
Row 2: P2, K2, (C2F twice) P2.
Row 3: as row 1.
Row 4: P2, (C2B twice), K2, P2.

Note: this plaited design looks stunning worked as a single panel down the front of a plain sweater. The first row is the wrong side of the patt.

Cable Check

Worked over 12 stitches, plus 6 stitches for repeat.

Row 1: (RS) P6 *K6, P6, rep from * across row.
Row 2: K6, *P6, K6, rep from * across row.
Rows 3, 7, 10, 12, 14, 16: as row 1.
Rows 4, 6, 8, 9, 11,15: as row 2.
Row 5: P6, *C3B, P6, rep from * across row.
Row 13: *C3B, P6, rep from * to last 6 sts, C3B.

Note: these instructions may look complicated, but they are simple to knit as many rows repeat. The pattern makes a good all-over design.

Index